KU-417-973

stuffed

by the same author

All It Takes
White Light
The Yellow Banana

stuffed

growing up in a restaurant family

patricia volk

BLOOMSBURY

First published in Great Britain 2002

Copyright © 2002 by Patricia Volk

The moral right of the author has been asserted

Photographs, unless otherwise noted, are from the author's personal collection.

Portions of this work were originally published in somewhat different form in the following: Allure; New York Times; New York Times Magazine; O, The Oprah Magazine; and Redbook.

Grateful acknowledgment is made to Sony/ATV Music Publishing LLC for permission to adapt an excerpted lyric from "Take Me Out to the Ballgame" by Albert Von Tilzer and Jack Norworth, copyright © 1908 by Broadway Music Corp. and Bienstock Publishing Co. (Copyright renewed). All rights on behalf of Broadway Music Corp. administered by Sony/ATV Music Publishing LLC, 8 Music Square West, Nashville, TN 37203.
All rights reserved. Used by permission.

Bloomsbury Publishing Plc, 38 Soho Square, London, W1D 3HB

A CIP catalogue record for this book is available from the British Library

ISBN 07475 5959 7

10 9 8 7 6 5 4 3 2 1

Printed in Great Britain by Clays Ltd, St Ives plc

The store

For Polly and Peter, with utmost love

The art of being wise is the art of knowing what to overlook.
— WILLIAM JAMES

CONTENTS

STUFFED

Sussman Volk, the man who brought pastrami to the New World
(Collection of the Lower East Side Tenement Museum)

Our hallway was the color of ballpark mustard. The living room was cocoa, my mother's wall-to-wall, iceberg green. The floor of the lobby was maroon-and-white terrazzo, like Genoa salami. When our elevator went self-service, the wood was replaced by enameled walls that looked like Russian dressing, the lumpy pink kind our housekeeper, Mattie, made by lightly folding Hellmann's mayonnaise into Heinz ketchup with a fork. Daisies were the fried eggs of flowers, gladioli the asparagus. We were a restaurant family, four generations in a six-block radius. When you opened our fridge, food fell on your feet.

The restaurant was at 141 West Thirty-eighth Street, in the heart of the garment center. Designers, models, and buyers buzzed in, looked each other over, and stopped by tables to say, "Hey there!" or "How long you in town?" They dressed to show what they were capable of. "Sir!" Dad said with a military snap, flaring open your menu. He'd pull your chair and straighten your salt and pepper shakers whether you were Pauline Trigère or not. "Gus!" He'd raise a finger. "Ice water at twenty!" He set a hard party rhythm. He table-hopped. He had a story for you. On the floor, because he was so tall, he floated above hunched diners and waltzing waiters wearing red weskits he designed.

The garment center was a ghost town on weekends, so Saturdays Dad worked half a day. Late in the afternoon he'd come home hoisting a corrugated carton on his shoulder precision-packed with two pounds of sliced turkey breast, sliced ham, sliced Swiss, a side of bacon cut into rashers, fat-marbled steaks wrapped like presents in waxed paper, a rack of lamb, round white cardboard containers filled with number 20 shrimps (twenty to the pound), almond crescents, strawberry tarts glazed with strawberry gelatin, brown bags of Vassilaros Brothers coffee, whole smoked fish the color of my grandmother's bangle bracelets, and Danish butter strip sold directly from the store to Nedick's, the only product Nedick's bought retail. Melons, string beans, celery like trees, cauliflower as big as the moon, pigs' feet in aspic, and a glass jar of pickled green tomatoes. A quart of Russian dressing, a quart of Roquefort, a pint of cocktail sauce. A brace of mahogany ducks with a quart container of Sauce Montmorency. And a quart of my father's famous Swedish mustard sauce:

    1. Take equal parts Düsseldorf mustard and sugar
    2. Add a little bit of oil and chopped chives
Those were the basics.

"Are you sick?" my mother would ask if I left a scrap from a twelve-ounce Delmonico. You weren't considered fed unless you were in pain. The more somebody loved you, the more they wanted you to eat. In a restaurant family, you're never hungry, you're starving. And you're never full, you're stuffed. When anyone rose from the table without a two-handed boost, my grandmother wailed, "Please, God, don't let him have gall-bladder!"

I couldn't walk down the street without running into someone whose hand-me-downs I wore, or who wore mine, or whose house I ate at, or someone I was glad to see even if it was only Nick the Popsicle Man, or Jimmy the old doorman, or Pat

the building driver who chauffeured us the two blocks to school
on days it snowed. Between Eighty-first Street and Eighty-
seventh, from Riverside Drive to West End Avenue, my aunts
and uncles lived, along with my great-grandparents, grandparents, friends, and even Benny, the man who sold penny candy,
sunflower seeds, chewable lips, and tiny wax bottles filled with
sugar syrup my sister told me would automatically fill up again if
I could just touch the bottom of one with a bobby pin and not
break it—an impossible thing to do.

M orgen's was the restaurant, but we called it the
store. It was the place I was a princess. Waiters
winked at me. They plucked the white linen napkin from under
my fork, twirled it high in the air, then draped it over my lap.
They nodded when I ordered, admiring my choices. They told
me jokes. And when I asked for a hamburger, my grandfather
would raise his forearm, then smash through the kitchen IN door
and grind a steak himself. On a good week I'd see my father
twice: Saturday afternoon, when he got back from the store. And
Sunday, our day. My sister and I would race to his bed, then
snuggle. We'd kiss his cheeks. He'd suck our earlobes, then turn
to my mother and say, "Audrey, I think this needs a little salt!"
He'd press the soles of his feet against our stomachs and
straighten his legs, and we'd be in the air, "Flying Angels." Then
Dad would drive us to woods, find a snake, and skin it. Or dissect
a chicken in the kitchen and explain how the pebbles in its crop
worked. Or we'd take the car to the Coney Island Freak Show
and gape at the Walrus Woman, the Leopard Lady, and the
Human Bullet, who was bald and had no arms and typed with
his toes. We'd eat pink cotton candy on paper cones, then throw
it up on the Tilt-a-Whirl. Starving, we'd head for dinner at
Charda's, Luchow's, or the Maharajah Room at The Pierre.
Before fusion cooking, before Austro-Asian, Afro-Shtetl, and
Thai-Inuit hit New York, most restaurants focused on the food of
a single country. In fancy places, it was served by people in
regional costumes, and you were serenaded with "Oh, Chichor-

neya," "Allez-vous En," or "The Mexican Hat Dance." You'd have to eat, listen, and smile while someone plinked a balalaika at you. If I misbehaved in the restaurant, my mother would walk me outside to where the car was parked and lock me in until the meal was over. I would breathe against the window and write words in my wet breath: ASS, BITCH, WHORE. When I got home, I would take out my Christmas Book, a small spiral notebook with a list of everyone I made presents for. I'd draw a black tree next to my mother's name, which meant one more Christmas she wouldn't get a gift.

"What did I do that was so bad I had to be locked in a car?" I ask my sister.

"You were . . . oppositional," she says, then adds with a voice full of sorrow, "I forgot about that."

At the height of her anger, the apex of her rage, my mother used to say she was sending us to Mrs. Brown's Orphanage.

"I don't believe you," I'd say.

"Is that so?" She'd pick up the phone and dial a number. My sister and I would listen in on the extension.

"Hello?" a woman's voice said.

"Hello, Mrs. Brown? This is Mrs. Volk, and my terrible daughters are acting up again."

"Oh really, Mrs. Volk?"

"Yes. Can I drop them at the orphanage tomorrow?"

Mrs. Brown would say why certainly, she had two empty beds, she'd be delighted to have us the very next day.

Although my sister was older, she'd burst into tears. She'd promise to be good. I was ready to go to Mrs. Brown's. If my mother didn't want me, I didn't want her. In my sixth-grade autograph book she wrote:

> *If all your friends desert you*
> *Pray don't look for another*
> *But come to the one who loves you best*
> *Your dearest friend, your mother*

Years later she told us her old friend Ruth Kahn had played the part of Mrs. Brown.

We were allowed to stare at freaks on Coney Island because they expected to be stared at. It was how they made a living. Staring at them was good for us. It would reinforce how lucky we were by sensitizing us to chance. But there were people in our neighborhood we had to pretend we didn't see. The Tongue Lady had a green tongue that hung down her chest then rolled up fast as a lizard's. On Broadway, the Glass Man had no legs and made music by tapping a spoon against eight glasses filled with graduated heights of water. One block north, the Organ Grinder seemed normal enough, but you could see every bone on his balding monkey. You gave the man whatever you had so the monkey wouldn't starve. The most terrifying person in the neighborhood was the Black Widow. She ate lunch at Schrafft's every day, a woman the size of a nine-year-old in turn-of-the-century widow's weeds. Her black boots laced above her ankles. Her skin was talcum white. She ate without taking off her broad-brimmed hat and veil. If she caught you staring, the Black Widow would raise the veil and spit at you.

Because it was only one block from my grandmother's apartment, we also ate at the Tip Toe Inn. When World War II was over, the day Uncle Bob got back from four and a half years on Saipan, that's where my grandparents took him for his first civilian meal. Four and a half years my grandmother wouldn't allow flowers in her apartment. Four and a half years my grandfather was retired from the restaurant business, refusing to buy black-market meat while his boy was overseas.

Uncle Bob studied the menu. He ordered turkey with stuffing, then took in the scene. The Tip Toe Inn was busy. People ate there all the time. They came at three in the afternoon for dinner because you could get the same meal at lunchtime prices. It was the kind of place you heard people eat and saw people talk. Uncle Bob looked around. For four and a half years he'd lived in foxholes. And here were people eating and laughing at the Tip Toe Inn. Uncle Bob raised his water glass, then put it down. His shoulders shook. Without a word my grandparents rose from their seats, linked their arms through his, and walked him home.

Since my mother only knew how to cook scrambled eggs and bacon, on Mattie's night off we'd eat at her mother's. I'd walk there straight from school and watch Lilly Brebner, the Jamaican housekeeper, singe quills off juicy nine-pound neutered roosters called capons on a gas stove. Seated around Nana's table would be my great-grandparents; my grandfather; Nana's older sister, Aunt Gertie, and Gertie's son, Wally; her younger sister, Aunt Ruthie, and Aunt Ruthie's husband, Uncle Albert; her older brothers, Uncle Jerry and Uncle Al; Uncle Bob and Aunt Barbara; and since somebody had to be at the store, my mother and my sister and me, but not my father.

At these meals my grandmother would force-feed my grandfather: "Eat, Herman, eat!" she'd beg. "Eat for *me*!" He'd throw his hands up: "No! Not another bite!" But despite his protests—"I can't!" "Polly, you're killing me!" "*Gutenyu*, I'm *dying*!"—she would drop another chosen morsel on his plate. The oyster of the capon, a clot of buttered toasted almonds from the string beans, the orphaned strawberry on the shortcake platter, a crimp of piecrust glossy with caramelized apple juice. "Eat! You don't eat enough! A man like you! You work so hard! Just the end piece, darling? For me, Herman, *please*?"

My grandfather was being fattened. It was painful to watch. I worked up the courage to complain about it. "You don't understand." My mother smiled. "He loves it. He wants that food. He wouldn't eat it if she didn't do that. He would never give himself the best part."

Not too long ago my sister and mother flew into town for the day. We planned to go to the Russian Tea Room for pelmeny (Russia's tiny veal-filled answer to the wonton), then catch a matinee. I made the reservation for noon. When we got to the restaurant, the line was out the door.

"We're never going to make curtain," my mother said.

"I really want that pelmeny," my sister said.

I pushed my way to the maître d' and explained the situation. I reminded him we had a reservation.

"I'm sorry." He shrugged. "There's nothing I can do."

"You see that woman?" I pointed to my mother. She was wearing a black cape with batwings and a high collar. It was chic, but it threw her gorgeous face into ghoulish shadow and made her neck disappear. "That woman was just *released* today. Right before we came here. She expected to be seated at noon. I can't vouch for what she'll do if she's not seated *now*."

The waters parted. We were whisked to a table. Three waiters pulled our chairs. The service was flawless. All of us agreed the pelmeny used to be better. As we were leaving, my mother turned to me and said, "What did you say to the maître d'?"

"I told him you were just released, Ma."

She laughed, not believing me.

On long Sunday trips in our red convertible, we'd stop at Howard Johnson's, where I had the clam roll. My sister and I sat in the back, but my mother would let me climb over if I said I was carsick. I'd press my feet against my father's thigh and drop my head in her lap, and she'd run her fingers through my short, curly hair, starting at the back of my neck. "My favorite place," she called the hollow there. I'd fall asleep to Lamont Cranston on the radio, the briny smell of tartar sauce on my fingers, and the sound of my mother whispering to my father, "Doesn't she have gorgeous hair?"

"Cecil" Sussman Volk (a.k.a. Stuff), around the time he invented the Six-color Retractable Pen and Pencil Set and the Hydraulic-powered Double-sided Garbage Can Brush

Move it, Lardass!" Dad shouts across the net. He's pissed. I have allowed a backhand to whiz past me in the alley when I should have been there "anticipating" the ball.

Being called Lardass used to make my eyes fill. Knucklehead and Turkey could do it too. Now I think it's touching Dad screams at me about my game. Since he had the meniscus removed from his left knee, he no longer moves laterally. He can go backward. He can go forward. Side to side is a thing of the past. I have to hit the balls down the center, or he storms off the court snapping, "Well, if you're going to play *that* way."

My father taught me how to swim, speak French, drive, eat using the utensils American-style (which nobody else in America seems to do), spot weld, solder, emboss, ride English, ride western, merengue, sing pop songs from World War I's "Keep Your Head Down Fritzie Boy" up through his favorite—the one that chokes him up, although he's not sure why—"Younger Than Springtime," remove a splinter, sap a blister by sticking a steril-ized threaded needle through it then tying the exposed ends in a knot, carve a Thanksgiving turkey, chop, dice, and mince, make canapés, deglaze a pan, suck meat off a lobster a lobster doesn't know it has, blind a mugger, kill a rapist with a rabbit punch, remove stains, cloisonné, and intimidate a tennis opponent by clenching my teeth then drawing my lips back and growling like a gas-station dog.

Things I've never heard from anyone else:

"A horse can't rear without taking a step backward first."

"Man is motivated by the Five P's: Pride. Power. Prestige. Possession. Preservation."

"Most people are members of the IGMFU Club: I Got Mine, Fuck You."

And whenever we go for clams: "Sailors chew steamer shells for calcium."

Then there's Dad's "The Bully on the Block" philosophy: "A little boy comes out on the street and a big bully comes along and starts punching him in the face. The little boy has three choices: He can stand there and take it, fight back, or go away. It's his decision to make." The Bully on the Block is summed up by Dad's credo: Nobody does anything to me. I do it to myself.

Seeing *The Alamo* with him at ten a.m. on Forty-second Street when I'm between jobs and the store is poised for lunch, my father shakes his head and says, "The Texas longhorn didn't come up from Mexico until 1847." He knows his stuff. Dad can tell, when we're eating beef, what the cow ate: grass or corn. If it was grass, what kind of grass: rye or wheat. If it was rye or wheat, if it was fresh or hay. Facts this precise, this knowledgeable, led me to men who flaunt the arcane.

My father sees his job as teacher. "Heels down! Toes in! Back straight!" he shouts when we ride. "Knees!" he barks. *"Knees, Knucklehead!"* From the moment Dad stands in one stirrup and swings his leg over, he is in command. He is boss. He rocks in the saddle as if riding is the way humans evolved to get around. Like Portuguese *rejoneadors,* he can ride without reins, controlling the horse with his knees.

I wear my pony-skin jacket to ride, a sort of warning. "See

this?" I lengthen my arm under the horse's muzzle, letting him sniff the skin. "You better be good." I want to be good for Dad. But no matter how much I trust him, I can't believe I can control 1200 pounds of flesh with my pinkies anymore than I can believe Lamaze will make childbirth painless or a tennis ball won't blind me if I play net.

My father learned to ride at the Pine Tree Stables in Prospect Park when he was six. James Sheriff, the family chauffeur, drove him there in the wicker rumble seat of a black Renault Cabriolet. Dad's early schools were the Aitz Chaim Yeshiva on Thirteenth Avenue and Fifty-fifth Street in Borough Park, P.S. 128, and the *shul* where his father was president, Tefrah Torah, at Eighty-third Street and Twenty-third Avenue. It was at Tefrah Torah that a rabbi punished Dad by locking him in a safe.

"Were you good after that?" I ask him.

"I haven't been in a safe since," he says.

When Dad was nine years old, that rabbi called him out of class. "You're wanted at home," the rabbi said, then nodded toward the door.

Dad knew his father was dead. To comfort himself, he rode the subway singing a song from his older sister's dance recital:

> *"Life is like a butterfly*
> *Da-da, dee-da, da-da-da"*

Jacob Volk had diabetes, but it was pneumonia that killed him. No antibiotics in 1929. He belonged to forty-eight philanthropic societies, but according to tradition, Jake was buried in a plain pine box. Gold coins were pressed over his eyes. Paid mourners wept, trailing his coffin through the streets of Bensonhurst, all the way to the Washington Cemetery on MacDonald Avenue. Dad spent the rest of the day watching the ice that preserved his father's body melt into the back lawn.

At twenty-nine my grandmother was a rich widow with three children. She sent my father to the Roosevelt Military Academy in Monsey, New York, where they forced him to become right-handed.

"It was a dumping ground for kids," Dad says. "Some of the boys were only five."

Roosevelt was run by Dr. Carrington, an Englishman who taught Latin with a .22 on his lap. When Dr. Carrington saw a squirrel, he'd open the window of his classroom and shoot it. Then he'd send a German shepherd named Mary out to crush its head. The students watched silently from their desks.

Summers Dad was sent away to Saratoga Springs, where he boarded with the Qwas, a Native American family, and got to ride. When he was thirteen, his mother shipped him off to the Valley View Dude Ranch in West Cliff, Colorado, to earn his spurs and learn cowboy skills he would never use again. There he was accidentally shot on two separate occasions. The city boy made his way in this strange land by telling jokes. He still tells jokes. He's compiling a joke book. Dad knows so many jokes, we play a game.

"All right," he says. "Give me a subject."

And I'll think of the most ridiculous thing I can. "Okay, Dad— *bubbles!*"

"Man walks into a bar with bubbles on his head," Dad begins. . . .

He likes to pretend he can't remember my birthday, July 16:

"Okay, Dad. When's my birthday?"

"I don't know."

"Think, Dad."

"Two days after Bastille Day?"

I grieved for the fatherless fact of my father's childhood. I loved him so much, loved everything about him—how he brought the cold in on his coat, the way the feather looked in the grosgrain ribbon on his fedora, the sweet oakey smell of his breath, riding his shoulders to watch the Veterans Day Parade, the strange things he knew that nobody else did. I wanted to be good at the things he tried to teach me purely to make him happy, to show him an excellent teacher produces an excellent student. But what I was good at wasn't what he taught. I could, for instance, do a perfect jackknife. I could get high, high,

high in the air and then beyond when it was reasonable, at the last possible moment, jack my hips and touch my toes, a human isosceles triangle. I could dangle in the air like a picture on the wall before deciding, Why not make the descent? I could ride my bike downhill with no hands. I could hold my breath in the pool for two laps. I was ruthless at Ping-Pong, spitting on the ball before I served. I had an inborn talent for rendering. I could draw anything. And I could imitate famous people. I could sing exactly like Eartha Kitt ("Daddy"), Jimmy Durante ("Inka-Dinka-Doo" and "Ya Gotta Start Off Each Day with a Song"), Al Jolson ("Swanee"), Ethel Merman ("There's No Business Like Show Business" and "Yes, I Can!"), Betty Boop ("I Wanna Be Loved by You"), Marilyn Monroe ("Happy Birthday, Mr. President" and "Diamonds Are a Girl's Best Friend"), and Carol Channing (also "Diamonds Are a Girl's Best Friend"). I wanted to make Dad happy. The idea was, if I could make him happy, I could somehow make it up to him that he'd grown up fatherless, shipped away, shot. Making him happy was my job. It's why I was born.

"He was nobody's boy," Mom says. "I would make him my boy."

Not growing up with a father, my father developed his own ideas about fathering. He committed himself to making sure I was fearless. If I could be cool in a crisis, I would survive. To that end, he pushed me so high on the playground swing, the chains went slack as it soared above the armature. This was supposed to make me not afraid of heights. Not being afraid could also save my life in a fire or flood. My parents had been traumatized by accounts of the Coconut Grove fire: 490 bodies piled up behind sealed doors in a Boston nightclub— a defining tragedy of the forties. My sister and I were drilled on how not to get trapped in a fire. Anytime we enter an enclosed public space, we are trained to look for the red EXIT sign and position ourselves as close to it as possible. If the movie or restaurant is crowded, we map with our eyes the path we'll take when our nostrils detect smoke. We were expected to leap off lifeguard towers at Long Beach from the time we were three in case we had to hurl ourselves out a window.

The best way to learn, according to Dad, is the hard way. Once you can do it the hard way, the normal way is a piece of cake. When I was five, he rowed to the middle of Schroon Lake in the Adirondacks and threw me overboard. Teaching me to drive, he insisted I master reverse before forward. "Anyone can go forward," he said. "I want you to back around the Zissus' driveway twenty times." Round and round we went in the neighbors' circular driveway until I mastered reverse. It was like trying to tie a bow in a mirror.

In a restaurant family you don't see your father much. It's not the glamorous business lay people take it for. Dad was in the store by six every morning to inspect meat and fish deliveries, check prices, and determine the daily menu. If broccoli was up, the vegetable of the day was steamed cauliflower with herbed bread crumbs sautéed in *beurre noisette* or zucchini with onions and stewed tomatoes. By six thirty he'd be on the phone with the menu printer. He got home around midnight after closing. I saw him on Saturdays at the exquisite hour when my sister and I would get back from the double feature at Loew's Eighty-third and Dad would be getting ready to go out, poking his studs in, sipping a Scotch, humming along with Lena Horne, George Shearing, or the La Playa Sextet on the radio. I'd sit on his bed and watch him take little dance steps, stretching his neck as he knotted his tie. I counted my clothes in food. If a new dress cost $32, that was two orders of Lobster Newburg and one Coconut Ball with Chocolate Sauce Dad had to sell.

I know my father's scars as well as my own: The ones from getting shot in Colorado. The lung surgery. The white-waled dent on his back where a Ford V-8 rolled over him while he was pushing it up a hill for his pal Herb Kronish, whose mother once told my father, "Slit my throat when I'm dead to make sure I'm dead." Knuckle and finger scars real restaurant men—the kind who can do any job in the kitchen—get. Some adolescent acne pits weekly radiation treatments couldn't cure. Several eyebrow gashes from various racquetball and motorcycle skirmishes, the fingertip dent from the time he cut the end off and I had to go downstairs and find it in the sawdust and bring it to the hospital in a cup of milk. "Look around the band saw," Dad said when he phoned home. "Try not to walk on it." And his two scars from nocardia, a rare disease that has nothing to do with the heart. Dad gets it from being pricked by the cacti around his house in Florida because he refuses to wear long pants.

G ood manners are important to my father. As a restaurant man he spent long hours watching customers eat the wrong way. We heard stories about people who used bread as a pusher or rested their knives with the blade on the plate and the handle on the tablecloth. We heard about women who buttered bread on their palms, or poured sauce from the gravy boat instead of ladling it. People who cut all their meat into pieces before they started, then pushed the plate away when they were finished. People who spooned their soup from the front of the bowl or made an X of their utensils or picked their teeth. Mr. B., the customer who washed his flatware in his water glass. The mogul who gesticulated with a fork. Dad once saw a customer stab a piece of meat with a steak knife, then put the knife in his mouth. We were horrified. My father has flawless manners even when he eats strange things. From a crystal bowl he spoons Heinz ketchup on hooves, cheeks, and pickled pigs' feet. He builds tiny tepees of chewed chicken bones on the rim of his plate. His favorite lunch these days is whatever's left over— yams, steak, corn, coleslaw—minced with ketchup in the Cuisin- art. No matter what goes in, it comes out gray.

W hen my parents move to Florida, Dad dupli- cates his studio from up north, down to the floor tiles that look like Lobster Cantonese sauce and the ceiling- high supermarket aisles stacked with bins of nails, drawers of screws, coiled wires, brads, bits, leather pieces, plastic ropes, bungees, rusty debris he calls "mongo" salvaged from construction sites, grommets, glazes, antique tools, new tools, oiled tools, dry tools, acetylene torches, families of screwdrivers, clamps, and vises, and yellow metal restaurant fillet of sole tins brimming with paints, gessoes, glues, electric switches, and findings, old license plates, phone jacks, tap and die sets. This is Dad's place, a place from which, if you had to, you could rebuild the modern world. It's where he does his sculpting and his fixing.

"Got anything that needs to be fixed?" he says, voice rich with fix-lust when I'm coming down to visit. This can be whatever— busted luggage, loose earrings, a stain on my favorite T-shirt. In the studio we put on soldering goggles, and he gets to tell me what I'm doing wrong. Our most recent project was making napkin rings out of copper tubing. I measured them, then marked the cuts with a grease pencil and used a heavy vise to hold the tubing while I sawed. I wanted to emboss the rings with personalized messages for each family member: EAT YOUR VEGGIES, USE THIS NAPKIN, YUM. To emboss, you have to tighten the copper in the vise, hold each letter down where you want it to imprint, then whack it with a sledgehammer. I was afraid I'd crush my thumb, so I lined up the letter, took my hand away, then hit it. Sometimes the letter jumped or didn't come out deep enough, and I'd have to reline it up and try again, which, unless I did it perfectly, gave the letter a drop shadow.

Dad watched. Steam shot out of his ears. He tucked in his lips and sucked air. "Chowderhead! That's not the way to do it. You want to do it the *right* way or *your* way?"

He lined up the letter, held it down with his fingers, and bonged it like John Henry. The letter came out deep and clear.

"I'm afraid I'll hit my fingers," I explained.

"You're not gonna hit your fingers."

"Well, anyway," I said, "I want these napkin rings to look man-made. I want them to have errors. I don't want them to look perfect, Dad."

"Don't worry."

Last year he taught me how to solder. I heated up the soldering iron, cleaned the copper with sulfuric acid, and carefully dripped silver onto the join. Dad stopped what he was doing to inspect the work. I rose from the workbench so he could slide onto my stool. He flipped down his Optivisors and held the solder under his fluorescent lamp. He pulled it. He twisted it. He knocked it against the vise, hit it with a hammer, then slammed it onto the floor.

"That's a good solder," he said.

When I was growing up and we lived in Manhattan, my mother liked to throw dinner parties. A typical menu would start with Shrimp Cocktail, then a salad, then Sautéed Veal Baked with Marsala and Cream, Rice Pilaf with Onions and Sultanas, and, in season, Asparagus Beurre au Citron. Dessert might be Baked Alaska Flambé or Chocolate Mousse in a crystal bowl lined with ladyfingers. But before all that, before the ice bucket was filled and the doorbell began to ring, my father would go into the kitchen and prepare the canapés. He'd pull a long white cook's apron over his head and tie it in the front. He'd roll up his sleeves. He'd stroke a ten-inch carbon steel chef's knife against a whetstone. He'd take three loaves of perfectly square, perfectly presliced black bread, butter them six at a time, then drape smoked salmon over the tops. When six were complete, he'd cut the bread on the diagonal and trim it. Slivers of smoked salmon would fall off with the crusts. "Open," my father would say. Like a baby bird, I'd bend my head back and open my mouth. He would laugh and drop the slivers on my tongue and only mine. My sister had been traumatized by a sea robin he caught when she was three and placed on her Mae West. She has never eaten fish since then and wears rubber gloves to prepare tuna salad for her husband. Mattie would be tidying up the guest bathroom and making sure the living-room cushions were plumped. My mother would be getting dressed. So my father and I were alone in the kitchen. And for the time it took to make three loaves of smoked salmon canapés, he was mine.

The Volk Girls with our beloved beagle, Morgen.
Together we've been on forty-four diets.

CHOCOLATE PUDDING

Beaming down the high school corridor, my big sister comes toward me. Why is she laughing so hard? Nearing her I can see: She is wearing my blouse. The blouse I saved up months to buy. The blouse I've never worn. She's stolen it out of my closet. If rage could kill, I would be dead.

Born eighteen months apart—both accidents—my sister and I fought daily. Knives were thrown. Ribs were kicked. My right thumb was slammed off in a door. Circle fights were the worst. Trapped in a room we'd hiss and snarl, grabbing weapons to maim with—hangers, hairbrushes, shoes—whatever you could reach without breaking the circle. Eventually my sister won. She always did. Then she'd pin me and drip spit on my face.

"Someday you'll love her." My mother would smile.

"I wish she was dead," I'd say.

And yet, and yet . . .

Punished together, banished to our room, instantly we were allies. We plotted escape. We wrote musicals and did the cancan. We midwifed black mollies and developed our own language: A penis was a linga-linga. A fart was a foogee. A pretty girl, a shpa-gooli, and an ugly girl, a bashalaga. When our parents spoke French so we wouldn't understand, we made up our own French:

> *Shock on voo shawn on tain.*
> *Instun tain on poo sha.*

On Sundays, when Mattie was off, we'd cook. "Let's make chocolate pudding!" my sister would say, and we'd race to the kitchen. She'd reach for a box of My-T-Fine from the pantry shelf, then take a bottle of milk out of the fridge. Cream rose to the top then. We'd use all of it, then pour the My-T-Fine into an aluminum pot. The stove was gas. When my sister lit the match, blue flames shot out of black holes toward the ceiling. I stood back. The whoosh could singe your eyebrows.

Since she was older, my sister would stir first. When she'd get bored, I'd stir and she'd tell me what I was doing wrong.

"You're going too fast!" "You're going too slow!" "You're going backward!" Mattie stirred in figure eights, rotating the pot so that every part of the bottom would get touched. But no matter what we did, the pot would scorch and the pudding would stick.

When you saw the first bubble, the pudding was done. We'd pour it into four-ounce Pyrex cups. While it cooled, we'd fight over the spoon. If you cared about quantity, the pot was more desirable. There was more pudding in the pot than the spoon, even if it tasted scorched. But usually the spoon was preferable because it had a well where the pudding was thick, even though it made the pudding taste like wood.

After we'd scrub the pot with Babbo, we'd take the pudding to our parents on a tray. They'd take a taste, say how good it was, then we'd get under their satin quilt. At some point during the snuggling, my sister would kick me or punch me or pull down my pajama bottoms.

"Why did you beat me up so much when we were little?" I ask her.

"What did you do that made me?" she replies.

Last weekend, on a trip to Florida to meet her second grandson, my sister glares at me over a grapefruit. "How could you send the baby that gift?" she smolders. "You sent Daniel a silver cup."

"I did?" I say. "I'm supposed to remember that?"

"How could you send Matthew a jumpsuit and rattles?"

"That jumpsuit came from a very good store," I say. "And the rattle thing had twelve rattles in it."

"They were *plastic*." My sister says the word like she's vomiting.

"I thought it was a great gift. It was two things and one of them had twelve things."

"Well, you should send Lizzie a silver cup for Matthew. That's what you sent when she had Daniel."

"Okay," I say. "Ask Lizzie to send me back the jumpsuit and the rattles, and I'll get him the silver cup."

"Girls! Girls!" my mother tsks from her chaise.

"For fifteen dollars more you could have given him a silver cup."

"A gift is a gift," I say. "Why do you have to measure it?"

"It's a terrible gift." My sister's eyes go dark.

"What do you think, Mom?" I ask. "You were with me when I got the stuff."

Mom thinks. "Actually, I thought you'd get several jumpsuits," my mother says.

"It cost me three hundred and eighty-five dollars to fly down here to meet that baby," I say. "I have to buy a silver cup too?"

I know some sisters who by choice only see each other Mother's Day, and some who will never speak again. But most are like my sister and me, treasurers of each other's childhoods, linked by volatile love, best friends who make other best friends ever so slightly less best.

The nicest thing my sister said to me in the first seventeen years of my life was, "Hey, you know, your legs really aren't so bad."

I can't see myself without seeing her. Thanks to my sister, I consider myself short. I may be five feet seven, but she's five feet nine. Since she's a great athlete, I'm not. When it was her turn to serve at volleyball, the game was over. I played right field with the glove over my nose, terrified a ball would hit it.

Despite our differences, people called us the Volk Girls. But my sister's athleticism, academic excellence, and skill at attracting boys forced me to forge my own path. I became a painter. I studied bees. I mastered a stringed instrument made out of goat bladder and had intense relationships with boys who wore torso T-shirts and passed urgent notes in the hall.

When I was lucky enough to join her magic circle, my sister kept things exciting in ways I never dreamed of.

"I'm bored." She'd yawn and people would scramble to amuse her.

On weekends she'd have three dates a night: the Date, the Late Date, and the Late Late Date. She was the party doll. I searched for soul. The months that separated us were the Grand Canyon. Or was it simply that we were sisters, doomed to polarities, modeling ourselves *against* each other? My sister is on the board of seven organizations. So I wear *Eau de Stay Away.* My sister puts on jewelry to go jogging. I wear the same thing leaving the house the cleaning lady wears coming in. My sister would never buy used furniture. I would never buy new.

I show her my three-dollar tag-sale chairs. I've screwed a walnut into the top of each one.

"Look." I point to the nuts. "Nature's finial."

At the moment I was screwing walnuts into chairs in New York, my sister was setting fake rubies into chairs in Coral Gables.

Two thousand miles apart, we both decide to get pedicures, and we both pick Redford Red.

When I slice off the end of my finger on a kitchen mandolin, my sister says, "I did the exact same thing on a mandolin last year!"

Being an older sister, she bandaged it herself and never bothered to tell me. Being the younger sister, I called her from the emergency room at Roosevelt Hospital, where the top hand surgeon in New York was taking care of me. Thanks to birth order, my sister has something I'll never have: a need to be brave.

"Do you realize we can do *anything*?" my sister says.

She's a scuba diver. So now I am too. Last month she got me kayaking. Now I'm a PADI-certified Open-water diver considering buying an Aquaterra.

This morning she called: "I want you to think about something."

"What?" I feel like I'm falling.

"I want you to take five days off and come down here and we'll kayak six hours a day."

Six hours a day? In a kayak? Can I do that? I'll have to ask my sister. Because she thinks I can do something, sometimes I can. On the other hand, sometimes I don't know what's really me or what's just not her.

Every morning she wakes up to a yellow Labrador retriever licking her lips. "Hobbesy! Hobbesy!" my sister squeals, kissing the dog back. Then they go into the bathroom and brush their teeth. Do I truly dislike pets or just not love them enough to share a toothbrush? It's hard to know, since my sister is my frame of reference.

Which doesn't mean she can't still make me nuts.

In a restaurant I wipe sleep out of my eye, and she gasps, "That's repulsive!"

"What?"

"Don't you realize what you're doing?"

"Well, excuuuuuse me. I had something in my eye."

We are sharing a Cobb salad. A huge bowl is between us. My sister is picking out the blue cheese. The blue cheese is vanishing. I wasn't going to say anything, but now she's fair game.

"That's disgusting!"

"What?"

"You're picking out all the blue cheese!"

"Oh, would you like more blue cheese?" She stabs some globs. "If you wanted more blue cheese, why didn't you say so?"

Walking through the woods last summer, we decide to take a shortcut through a bog. Twenty minutes into it my sister and I realize we've made a mistake. Phragmites grass, ten feet tall, has enveloped us. If you stick your arm out, you can't see your hand. There's no turning back, because we don't know where back is.

"I can't do it," I whimper.

"Yes, you can!"

"Let's just scream."

"No one'll hear us."

"I can't walk another step."

"Come on! Try this!" That's when my sister, the Mensa member, invents the Way to Walk Through Phragmites. She locks her arm around my waist, then clamps mine around hers. She demonstrates how to stick your leg in the air, then form an arc with it. Legs synched, we sweep the stuff down one exhausting step at a time.

"We're never gonna make it," my voice wavers.

She laughs. "If I die first, you can eat me."

On a trip to New York we visit our old apartment. "Was it hard to swing?" my sister asks.

"Piece of cake. I sent a letter 'To the Occupants of 4E.' I sprinkled it with phrases like 'Mem'ry! That strange deceiver!' "

My sister laughs.

In front of the building we pause on the sidewalk. This is where we learned to roller skate, play hopscotch, jump rope, and ride our bikes.

"Who was the doorman who gave us Life Savers?"

"Tom. Who was the elevator man who borrowed our comics?"

"Jimmy."

Inside the lobby I study the bench where she once made me wet my pants by blocking access to the elevator.

"Who was the super with the German shepherd?"

"Mr. Korber. Who was the doctor with an office in the lobby?"

"Dr. Port."

Then the elevator reaches four, and we are standing in front of our old front door.

"Remember when you locked me out?" I say.

"Yeah." My sister sounds wistful. "Remember when you sleepwalked to the neighbors, and they found you on their toilet?"

"The Walds. They had angels on the wallpaper."

We ring the bell. A wary couple opens it, and from zero miles per hour I break into racking full-fledged sobs.

"Excuse me," I say. "I have no idea why this is happening."

"It's all right." They look worried.

"Omigod!" My sister looks around. "It's exactly the same!"

"Well, we ripped up that horrible brown linoleum in the foyer somebody put in," the woman says.

That was our linoleum, state-of-the-art.

"May we see the kitchen?" I ask.

In the kitchen my sister says again, "It's exactly the same!"

Not to me. It looks tiny. Everything looks tiny. But I was turning twelve when we left, and my sister was full-grown.

"Remember the time I pretended to commit suicide behind this door?" she says.

"Yeah, but you forgot to hide the Heinz ketchup."

We double over laughing. The people move closer to each other.

In the pantry, we automatically go right. Mattie's room is a storage closet now. I'd forgotten the wall behind her bed was made of privacy glass. Must have been to let light in, since her window overlooked an air shaft.

In the playroom, there are picture moldings I never noticed.

"Remember when we watched Lux Video Theater in here?"

"We did everything in here."

In the hallway leading to our mother's room, my sister says, "Remember when I crashed through the glass door?"

"Weren't you chasing me?"

The bedroom, which had the same trellised wallpaper Ozzie and Harriet's had, is peacock blue now, but the bed's in the same place.

"I used to love when we were sick and got to spend the day here."

"I used to love when Mom let us try on her green velvet robe."

"I used to love the way she rubbed Vicks in my chest for growing pains."

"I used to love the way she played with my hair after a shampoo. She dried it with her fingers. It took hours. Hours and hours and hours."

"You always had short hair," my sister says. "It took five minutes to dry."

The people are following us from room to room. I see pure relief on their faces when we start thanking them for the visit. Then I realize I haven't seen our old bathroom. I used to think there was treasure behind one of the tiles because it sounded hollow when you rapped it with your knuckles.

"May I use the bathroom?" I say.

There's a pause. They're not happy. Reluctantly they follow me to the bathroom. I smile at them and shut the door. I rap on the tiles. Still hollow. I flush the toilet.

Downstairs, I tell my sister I wish she could stay in New York a little longer, that next time she comes, we'll visit our playground.

"When we're older, we'll have more time for each other," she says.

"The best arrangement for elderly people is two siblings living together," I say.

"When our husbands are dead and we're just trouble to our kids, we'll still have each other," she says.

So I tell her this Greek thing. "It's ancient Greece," I say. "Your house is on fire. Your mother and father are in it. And your child, husband, and sister. Who do you save?"

"Your child," my sister says. "Of course, your child."

"Wrong! You can always get another child."

"Your parents?"

"Nope! Your parents are at the end of their lives anyway."

"Your husband, so you can make more children?"

"No way! You can always find another husband. According to the ancient Greeks, you save your sister. That relationship is irreplaceable. You can never have another sister."

"That's a classic example of sophistry," my sister says. "Reasoning that seems okay but leads to a false conclusion. Yeah. Definitely. That's sophistry. I think I remember that. The Greeks were famous for it."

The phone rings at 6:30 a.m.

"Hullo? Hullo?" No one is there. I know it's my sister.

"Coffee too hot?" I ask.

"Ummm," she squeezes out.

I take the portable into the kitchen and put my coffee up too. We'll talk about yesterday. We'll talk about tomorrow. We'll talk about our parents, our men, our kids, our work. We'll talk about our weight, the wisdom of keeping a food diary, how good veggies poached in broth can be and whether we should go to a spa.

"You can have real coffee at the Birdwing Spa in Minnesota," I'll say.

"Yeah, but you have to go to Minnesota."

"The Regency House Spa is near you. I'd come down."

"I can't live a week with no animal products."

"What about the Kripalu?"

"It has cinder-block walls, and they don't let you talk during meals."

"Know anything about the Tennessee Fitness Spa?"

"Is that, by chance, in Tennessee?"

We talk till she has to leave to see a patient or another call comes through, or I have to meet my walking friend. We talk every day. Although her take on our past is fixed in amber and mine has no membrane, she's my memory. There are things only we know. It was she who taught me how to smoke and hide the evidence and bunch socks in my bra. When I woke my mother to tell her "I think I got my period," in the Jewish tradition, she slapped my face, then mumbled, "Do you know what to do?"

"Yes." I lied, then asked my sister. It was my sister who taught me the facts of life by reading *From Little Acorns* nightly. It was she who beat me up when I howled at the good parts, then kept vigils with me by our bedroom window, waiting for the woman across the alley to take her nightly shower.

D o I trust her? Does she trust me? I keep a pound of the coffee she loves in my freezer. "I've got your coffee," I remind her when she calls to say she's coming. Always she packs her own can.

I don't know if I could live without my sister. Picturing life without her is not possible. I love her as much as I love me. *Ma soeur, c'est moi.*

W e decide to definitely diet. To launch it, we leave the world behind and head for three nights at a spa. No sooner do we turn into the driveway than my sister is making friends. She makes friends with the doorman, she makes friends with the bellhop, she makes friends with all the waiters and the startled funk aerobics instructor she drags into a corner and thumps her abs at. I hide and I shrivel, I shrink and I pale.

"Why do you have to make friends with everybody?" I ask.

"Why are you so unfriendly?" she says.

On the nature hike I'm last, she's first. She scales the Ice Glen singing. People keep running back down the mountain to check on me, "Are you okay?" "Are you sure you're okay?" At night, after dinner, my sister asks the waiter for two fat-free hot fudge sundaes to take back to our room, where she will simultaneously watch a video and return nine calls from patients who can't live without her. Then "What happened?" my sister asks about the movie, and I have to break the spell to fill her in. Then she makes a few more calls, and she's ready to turn out the light. Then she wants to talk. Then she wants to sing Patience & Prudence's "Tonight You Belong to Me" in the dark. (I'm melody. She's harmony.) Finally the Volk Girls are ready to sleep.

"Good night, *really*." We laugh, and that's when I hear it. It's the sound my sister has always made at night, a sound nobody else makes, a hard swallow that ends with a push of air out her nose.

Something opens. Something closes. Something opens again.

I used to time my breaths to hers. Open, close, open. The sound of her breathing is the sound I fell asleep to the first twelve years of my life in the blue room we shared with organza drapes that met like bosomy aunts bending over to kiss us, the room I still dream of, the room I still long for, separated by a night table, one arm's length from the person Siamesed to my soul—my sister, my half, my beloved Jo Ann.

Friday night at Great-grandma's. Back row (left to right): Jerry Lieban, Herman Morgen, Jenny Geiger Lieban, Dad, Albert Wolko. Front row (left to right): Gertrude June Lieban Shultz, Polly Ann Lieban Morgen, Dr. E. Alan Lieban, Mom, Louis Lieban, Ruth Helen Lieban Wolko (Note: The three sisters have the same hairdo.)

LAPSANG SOUCHONG

I loved my family because they were family, separate from their behavior in the world or how they treated me. They were mine, I was lucky to have them. Their stories were my history, and their histories were spoken of with reverence. In 1888 a paternal great-grandfather brought pastrami to the New World. In 1916 a grandmother took home the trophy for "Best Legs in Atlantic City." My grandfather won the land for his house in a card game with Jimmy Walker and was eulogized in *The New Yorker* by E. B. White. My father invented the first Hydraulic-powered Double-sided Garbage Can Brush, the Double-sided Cigarette Lighter so you never have to worry about which side is up when you go to light, the first Illuminated Lucite Single-shaft Fender Guide, which clamped to your fender and facilitated nighttime parking by showing you where your fender ended, the first See-thru Wristwatch, and the Six-color Retractable Pen and Pencil Set. (He was sold out by his partner, the mention of whose name in our family is still followed by spitting.) Dad opened the first frozen-food store in Greenwich Village, Penguin Foods. With a war going on, he figured working women would buy frozen food so they wouldn't need to market every day. My mother was president of the Junior League for Child Care. Everyone was a star in the family galaxy, even Aunt Gertie, whose husband gambled away her money, then died, forcing her to sell dresses at Sachs, not Saks. Aunt Gertie had perfect posture.

I loved my family because they were Morgens or Liebans or Volks. We were part of each other. So I loved Uncle Al, even though he cheated on his wife. Uncle Al sat back and watched while his sisters scurried to please him. He wove his forearms over his chest, puffing his pipe like a chieftain while they kept his glass filled. Uncle Al was emotionally immune. He tolerated us. If he could say it the hard way, he did. This passed for genius.

An endodontist, Uncle Al was our family's only "professional." In that capacity he was our liaison to the medical world. When anyone had a health problem, even if it had nothing to do with teeth, they called Uncle Al for a referral. He knew the best rheumatologist, the best chiropodist, the best lung man. Uncle Al was famous in our family for two other things as well: the ability to write two different thoughts on a blackboard at the same time—one with his left hand, one with his right—and that he, and he alone, did Erich Maria Remarque's root canals. When you have someone in your family who sets you apart, that person's name is rarely mentioned without his credentials. Uncle Al was Uncle Al Who Could Write Two Different Thoughts on the Blackboard Simultaneously. And Uncle Al, Erich Maria Remarque's Endodontist. I was impressed, even if I didn't know who Erich Maria Remarque was and whether Erich Maria was a man or a woman.

Uncle Al didn't smile, wore a bow tie, and was the eldest of the five remaining Lieban children. He was Dr. E. (for Elias) Alan Lieban, pronounced *lee*-ban, the German way, even though it was spelled *lie*. Lie-ban, a ban on lies. It was a name to live up to, a name meaning truth. But Uncle Al was far from truthful. After dinner Thursday nights at my grandmother's, I'd slide under the table and eavesdrop. Uncle Al was having an affair with a Miss Dorsey. The name Lieban meant *lieb ban* then, a ban on love in a loveless marriage. Names so often meant something: Uneeda Biscuit; My-T-Fine pudding; Dr. Chargin, the dermatologist on Central Park West who didn't charge Aunt Gertie because she was poor.

W hen I was twelve, someone punched me in the mouth. A few days later the tooth that took the brunt of it started to ache. Then it throbbed. When it turned gray, my mother made an appointment with Uncle Al.

His office was in a penthouse on Central Park South. "You must be Patty," the nurse said, opening the door. "I'm Miss Dorsey. How do you do?"

Miss Dorsey! She worked for Uncle Al? I imagined she'd look like Marilyn Monroe, but Miss Dorsey had hair like the man on the Quaker Oats box. She wore a white nurse's hat and uniform, and laced white heels. "I believe the doctor is expecting you." She smiled.

"Oh, Dr. Lieban!" She knocked on a dark paneled door. "Dr. Lieeee-ban, your grand-niece is here!"

We waited. The knob turned. And there was Uncle Al in a side-buttoned barber's smock. It had a waistband and flared at the hips.

"Welcome." He nodded, but he didn't kiss me. Away from my grandmother's table, he looked older. "Some tea, Miss Dorsey," he ordered without looking at her.

I'd never been in a room alone with Uncle Al. I knew him solely from my grandmother's and rare outings to visit his Airedales in Wappingers Falls.

"Do sit." He extended his palm.

We waited for the tea in his dark, book-lined study overlooking the zoo. Uncle Al sat behind his desk. I searched my brain for something to say to a man brilliant enough to write two thoughts on the blackboard simultaneously and treat Erich Maria Remarque: What were my great-grandparents like when you were young? How come you never had children? Why does everyone hate Aunt Lil? Do you and Miss Dorsey do it *here*?

Uncle Al shuffled papers. He didn't look up. The light from his desk lamp cast wild eyebrow shadows on his forehead. He read tracing words with his finger so his shiny head snapped side to side. Could he read two thoughts at the same time too?

M iss Dorsey came in with a tray. She set it down on Uncle Al's desk. I watched to see how he looked at her. He didn't. I believed that people who were having sex wanted to whenever they were together. That wild current passed between them. But Uncle Al spoke to Miss Dorsey in a dismissive way, as if she were a servant.

The room filled with the smell of burnt rubber. I had never had tea before. Tea was for the elderly. Coffee would stunt your growth. The hot drink for children was cocoa. Uncle Al continued reading while steam curled out of the spout. I wondered what he had looked like when he and his brother Uncle Jerry ran away from home to become song-and-dance men. I tried to picture Uncle Al with a straw boater and cane. I tried to imagine him smiling. I put him in a striped blazer. Now he was edgy with disdain, a bald man with sunspots all over his head.

T he terrible smell filled the room. Uncle Al's chair faced me, blocking the window. There was nothing to look at except the bookshelves and him. The smell was so bad, I started breathing through my mouth.

"Tea?" he said finally.

"Yes, please."

"As a member of the American Academy of Dentistry, you must understand I cannot endorse the use of sugar," he said. "And milk obfuscates the taste of tea. In China, as you may or may not know, they never use milk and sugar in tea."

"Really?" I was intrigued.

"Do you know what tea is called in China?"

I'd read *The Good Earth* by Pearl S. Buck, but couldn't remember if it was in there. I shook my head. Uncle Al was not pleased.

"Cha," he said.

Black liquid streamed from the spout. Uncle Al handed me an ivory-colored cup with a gold rim. I decided to echo whatever he did. He flattened a napkin in his lap. He blew on the surface of his cup. He took a small slurp. The taste had a metallic edge, like blood. A bitter smoky taste too. I shut my nose down the way people do when they swallow medicine so they can't taste it.

"Lapsang Souchong," he said, raising his cup as if making a toast.

I rested mine on the saucer in my lap. There was no way I could take another mouthful. Uncle Al had an Oriental carpet. As he sipped his tea, I pretended to cough and, bending over, drizzled the contents of my cup onto the whirling blue and maroon pattern on the floor. The tea sank right in. Then I raised the cup to my lips and pretended to drink.

"Do you like Lapsang Souchong?" Uncle Al peered over the rims of his bifocals.

"Yes, thank you."

"Would you like some more?"

"No, thank you."

He rested his back against his chair and said, "Do you know what I do?"

"You're an endodontist."

"Do you know the difference between *endo* and *exo*?"

Another test, like cha. I knew Uncle Al wouldn't just be judging me, he would be judging my mother, who produced me, and my grandmother, who produced my mother. He would be judging my school, P.S. 9, and the entire public school system. He would be comparing me to his other grand-nieces and -nephews, including my smart sister. If I failed the endo/exo test, I failed for everyone. I didn't know the difference between endo and exo. The only Latin I was familiar with was *E Pluribus Unum*.

Endo/exo. I started to panic. Were endo and exo like arrival and departure? Is it the *plane* that's arriving or the *people* arriving to take the plane? Does departure mean people are departing on the plane, or that people who have arrived on the plane are departing and going home? Was daylight saving time fall forward, spring back? Or fall back, spring forward? When you trip, you fall *forward*. When you spring back, you *recoil*. But when you fall back in a line, you're *back* in line. And when you lunge, you *spring forward*.

Uncle Al waited for the answer. I thought hard, and then, as I so often did in school, I took a stab based on nothing, or worse, took a stab that was the opposite of what I thought was right because I was so often wrong: Uncle Al was an endodontist. He worked on root canals, which were *in* the tooth. So *en* meant *in*. But he took the roots *out*. Exit shows the way *out*, so endo was *out*. But the root was *in* the tooth, and that's where he worked, so *en* equals *in*. *En* sounds like *in*. Yeah! No! Too obvious, it must be wrong! Uncle Al wouldn't quiz me if it was that easy. Besides, if three outs *ended* an *inning*, maybe *en* meant out.

"Endo is out," I said, feeling like the cartoon character who runs off a cliff and treads air until NONG! It realizes there's no ground beneath its feet.

"No." Uncle Al sighed. "Endo is in, exo is out."

That was it. I was short on smarts, a marked girl.

Although having a root canal in my mouth annoys me every day of my life, the work he did has held up since the fifties.

Aunt Lil went through life thinking she got the small half. If you gave her flowers, she thought they were wilted. When you brought soup, she found a hair. The butcher shortchanged her. Empty cabs passed her by. She was a self-made outcast, and sooner or later everybody failed her.

You never knew if Uncle Al was going to be at my grandmother's Thursday dinners, and if he did come, whether he'd be there with Aunt Lil. Sometimes Uncle Al came alone. Aunt Lil wasn't blood. She'd married into the family. The room went quiet when she walked in. The sisters rolled their eyes at her baroque fingernails. Further proof of Aunt Lil's not fitting in was her astonishing challah hair—braided, wound, and woven. The sisters wore their hair short and black with a blond streak in the front. Unlike the sisters, who favored plastic pearlized harlequins, Aunt Lil wore pince-nez. Like the sisters, she dressed only in black, but instead of new jewelry, she favored dangling garnet earrings, brooches on skewers, watches on pins. Aunt Lil's jewelry was not purchased from the family jeweler, David of Dagil in

Lillian Berger Lieban made a needlepoint pillow
for her couch that read, I'VE NEVER FORGOTTEN
A ROTTEN THING ANYONE HAS DONE TO ME.

the diamond district, who specialized in new, shiny, and big. Aunt Lil preferred old gold that came with a story: who it belonged to, where she got it, how much she paid, what the auction was like, what she was sorry she didn't get at the auction, how the waste from a garnet was ground to dust, then used to make emery boards. She struck me as a freethinker. Is that what bothered the sisters?

If you told Aunt Lil you liked something, she unclasped it and gave it to you.

"What a pretty ring, Aunt Lil!"

"It's a peridot, darling. Here."

She'd slip it on my finger.

"Aunt Lil, I've never seen a bracelet like that!"

"Alexandrites, darling." She'd pinch the catch closed on my wrist. "Swear to me you'll use the chain guard."

Uncle Al slept with Aunt Lil for eleven years, then refused to marry her because she wasn't a virgin. She sent out wedding invitations anyway, and his mother, my great-grandmother Jenny Geiger Lieban, told him, "Al, you either go through with it, or you never see her again," so he did both. He went through with it, and he stopped seeing her. After the ceremony, Uncle Al rented an apartment at the Normandie on Riverside Drive, and Aunt Lil moved upstate to Wappingers Falls. They never had children. They had joint custody of the Shagzies, Airedales Aunt Lil tweezed instead of cut. There was a series of Shagzies—Shagzy the First . . . Shagzy the Second. . . . They all looked the same, and as each Shagzy died, he was replaced by a new Shagzy, like the Lassies on TV. Uncle Al would add the newly dead Shagzy's ashes to the urn shelf in his closet. When he got dressed, there were the urns. Even with the Shagzies dead, Uncle Al spent more time with them than with Aunt Lil.

I felt sorry for Aunt Lil. Although Uncle Al was unfaithful to her, no one in the family chastised him. What was ours was wonderful. Aunt Lil wasn't ours. The first time I heard the sisters light into Aunt Lil, I had no preparation for duality. I was struck by how they pretended to like her when she was around, but out of earshot, they pounced. The gripes were first and foremost that Aunt Lil was a lousy housekeeper. "So help me"—the sisters would raise a right hand as if they were in court—"I wouldn't eat there if my *life* depended on it!" Aunt Lil was also accused of not making Uncle Al happy. She spent his money on antiques. She didn't take care of him. Her biggest sin? Dirt under her finger-nails. This was particularly chilling because I had the same prob-lem. Did people talk about me when I left the room? On Sundays my father would inspect us: "Let me see your hands." I'd hold them out as if they were for sale. He'd study my fingernails, each one capped by a curved black parenthesis, and shake his head. "Are you in the real estate business?" he'd say.

I tried to keep my nails clean. I kept them as short as a hair. But even if I cleaned them with a damp orange stick (a nail-specific beauty aid from the five-and-ten with a pointy end for cleaning and a chiseled end for cuticle pushing), even if I cleaned them right before going to bed, they were black when I woke up. I took to wondering if Aunt Lil and I gave off some electromag-netic charge that attracted nail dirt.

Once a year Aunt Lil came to the city, and we'd take Shagzy to the dog show at the old Madison Square Garden. She'd wear a black hat and dress and laced black pumps that had an orthopedic authority. I was proud of her. She looked professional. Every year I was sure Shagzy would win. Aunt Lil had solid faith too. But always the Shagzies screwed up, breaking into a trot when they were told to walk or folding up when the other dogs hung turns. Shagzy and Aunt Lil would be fine in the grooming area. Aunt Lil, doing some last-minute fur fluffing, proudly pinning her number on, flushed as if she were going to a dance. Shagzy, thrilled to be out of his travel crate, sniffing poodles sculpted like cauliflowers, high-stepping past King Charles spaniels and perky chows, dog busy. But when it was time to go into the ring, Shagzy would sense something was up. His stubby tail would clamp down. He'd dig his forepaws in. The leash would get taut, and Aunt Lil would plead. Eventually she'd gather up the current Shagzy and carry him to his position in the ring. She'd repeat the commands as the judges barked them. "Heel!" she'd squeal in her cheese-grater voice. "Heel, Shagzy-boy! Heel! Heel! *Heel!*" But the Shagzy would bolt, skid on his rear, or flash his sharky teeth. Hairs burst from Aunt Lil's braid. Sweat grooved her powder.

Shagzy and Aunt Lil got disqualified in the first round every year. But Aunt Lil never reproached the Shagzy. She consoled him, loved him up, loved him to bits, maybe even loved him more for being so imperfect, so human. She told the Shagzy not to worry, that he was marvelous, that she adored him anyway. Would he like a cube of Muenster? How about a Liv-A-Snap? What a good boy he was! Yes! What a good puppy-lup! Such a lovebug! Yes! Oh, yes! That's my Shagzy-wagzy! That's mama's Shagzy-boy!

Shagzy wagged his tail stump. Aunt Lil raised her chin for a lick.

Aunt Lil's adult shoe size was three and a half. This enabled her to buy her shoes where I did, at Indian Walk on Broadway or a couple of blocks south at Rappoport's on Eighty-third, where your feet got fluoroscoped to make sure the shoes really fit. You'd stand on the machine and look through the eyepiece and see if there was breathing room for your toes. You'd see your white bones and gray skin and the dark leather curve of the toe box.

Aunt Lil liked Mary Janes, same as I did, same buckled strap, same grosgrain bow. Her feet were a matter of enormous pride. She favored white stockings to set off the shiny black patent. She liked to pull the skirt of her dress at the hips, then point and flex. Her hair was remarkable for its length and the intricacy of its braid, but no other grown-up had feet like that. Aunt Lil was just over five feet. She was heavy. Microfeet in little-girl shoes had the potential of giving her an air of instability. She could have looked unbalanced, like a ham on top of a pea. But standing still, Aunt Lil looked planted. There was nothing fragile about her except her wounded look.

When Uncle Al asked her for a divorce, she told him if he ever tried to leave her, she would throw acid in his face. This was around the time the investigative journalist Victor Riesel had acid thrown in his face by a teamster. From that day on, Victor Riesel was blind.

The Normandie was only three blocks from our apartment, so when Aunt Lil came to town, I'd visit. She'd give me milk and graham crackers and paint pens she saved only for me—the artist in the family—a set of clear plastic tubes with sponges at the tips. You filled the tubes with paint powder, added water, and shook them. The paint soaked down into the sponge, and then you pressed it into the paper and painted. Tinting power was minimal, and no matter how much pigment you used, the colors looked faded. I would offer Aunt Lil a wet picture before I left.

"Who's getting *that* one?" She'd point.

"My mother."

"That's the one *I* wanted," she'd say.

Finally, Aunt Lil made the whole family permanently turn on her. Since she was living up in Wappingers Falls, after Uncle Al's funeral my grandmother held the shivah. Aunt Lil rang the doorbell, took one look at the cakes, the turkeys, the chafing dishes. The petits fours, dried fruits, and capons. The herring, smoked salmon, and bagels. The cheeses, the cookie platters, the Everest of chopped liver. She took it all in, turned to my grandmother, and said her last words to our family, "My husband dies, and you throw a party?"

Eight years after her excommunication, I sent her a note: "Dear Aunt Lilly," it said. "I just got married, and I'd love to introduce you to my husband. May we come sometime and visit?"

It was a modest house, smaller than I remembered, filled with wending cats, empty jars, and piles of old newspapers she said she was "saving for the Boy Scouts." The papers were nervous-making. They leaned against the walls of her porch, buckling the screens. Near the bottom, they were dark as coffee. Higher up, they got creamy. Newspaper flakes littered the floor. Cat hair swirled in the air. There was a gray tabby in a Budweiser carton with newspaper crumbs in his fur and a calico on a sweater under the rocker. The smell was old damp paper and cat. Aunt Lil had shrunk. Her center part was pink. When I asked if she still had a Shagzy, she threw her head back. "Oh, I'm too old to have a dog." She laughed.

Because Aunt Lil's parents were from Hungary, she made something no one else in our family made. Spaetzle looked like dry scrambled eggs, but it was chewy like gnocchi. Even though she kept her house dark, light bounced off the melted butter. She cooked chicken paprikash to go with the spaetzle. The sour cream was so thick, the chicken beneath the sauce had the soft curve of foothills.

I watched Aunt Lil make the spaetzle. She reached into a bowl with her long, curved fingernails and curled the raw dough into her fist. Then she pumped her fist, working dough out the small hole at the pinkie end. She'd squeeze her hand, and a yellow worm would emerge. Then she'd clip it off with the thumbnail of her other hand and let it fall into a pot of boiling water. She had a rhythm: Dip. Squeeze, clip, squeeze, clip, squeeze, clip. Dip. When all the spaetzle rose to the top of the salted water, Aunt Lil drained the pot. I've seen only one other person turn their fist into a cooking utensil. My father uses his left hand like a pastry tube to drizzle icing into "Happy Birthday."

The spaetzle was good. Styrofoam would have been good with all that butter and sour cream. One of the cats jumped onto the table and ate out of the serving bowl. "Such a naughty boy!" Aunt Lil strummed behind his ears.

After lunch we sat in her living room on a carved oak bench with a high back and velvet cushions that had tassels the size of cantaloupes. It looked like something out of *King Lear*. We talked.

"Why do you keep calling me Aunt *Lilly*?" she interrupted, peeved. "I've never been a Lilly," and I realized I was confusing Aunt Lil with my grandmother's Jamaican housekeeper.

"Oh, I'm sorry," I said. "It's been such a long time. I guess I was mixing you up with Lilly Brebner!"

Aunt Lil shook her head. It was the wrong thing to say. I'd confused her with a housekeeper, and I'd referenced her arch-enemy, my grandmother. I didn't believe in inheriting family feuds, but felt disloyal anyway. My grandmother would not have liked that I was visiting Aunt Lil.

The sun went down. Aunt Lil asked us to stay over. I helped her make up a cannonball bed. I was fastidious about the hospital corners, not wanting to give her any reason to complain about me, even though there was no one left to complain to. We smoothed the sheets. Reaching for the satin quilt that all the women in the family bought from Mr. Oswald, the linen man who made house calls, I spoke. "Aunt Lil," I asked her, "how come you stayed married to Uncle Al when he treated you so badly?"

"Humans value what is hardest to attain, dear."

"How come you never had children?"

"Your Uncle Al never wanted children."

"Then how come you never worked?"

"He wouldn't hear of it."

Was Aunt Lil happy only when she wasn't happy?

Despite protests, when we left the next day, she gave us twenty-four gilt-edged oyster plates. She wrapped them in a HIN-DENBERG EXPLODES! newspaper and sent us on our way.

The next year she made us stuffed cabbage with rice and almonds. The newspaper collection had grown. So had the flaky cats in corrugated beer cartons and sweater nests.

"Aunt Lil," I asked her, "what was it with you and Aunt Ruthie?"

"She knew I knew how old she really was."

"And you and Aunt Gertie?"

"There is no evil. There are only human beings."

Then she went upstairs and came down with a tazza. It was crystal, engraved in diamond point, with a trumpet-shaped foot. My husband and I were crammed into a studio apartment. The tazza bore no relation to our way of life.

"No, Aunt Lil. Really. I can't."

She glared at me over her pince-nez and said, "You need a tazza for sweetmeats, dear."

Two years went by, and we drove up with a baby.

"What are your neighbors like?" I asked her.

"If you don't read the *Reader's Digest,* there's nothing to talk about."

"Do you read the *Reader's Digest*?"

"No."

This time we had goulash. A new cat jumped on the table and lapped her plate. Aunt Lil wrapped twelve stem cordials commemorating the Battle of the Boyne in a newspaper.

"Please, Aunt Lil. We don't drink cordials."

"Don't tell me what I can give you!"

On her couch were two pillows done in needlepoint. One said, HOPE FOR THE BEST. EXPECT THE WORST. The other, I'VE NEVER FORGOTTEN A ROTTEN THING ANYONE HAS DONE TO ME.

When the next baby came, we drove up again. This time we brought lunch, her favorite: sturgeon sandwiches from Russ & Daughters.

"I told you I wanted *rye,*" she said. "Not egg bread." I could see she thought I had done it on purpose, done it to be cruel. I asked after her nephew.

"People keep giving themselves away, dear," she said. "That's how we learn about them."

I asked what her happiest memory was.

"It was the day my brother pushed me out of the apple tree. My arm broke in three places. That night Mother permitted me to sleep in her bed."

Then she gave us the epergne.

"I can't take this, Aunt Lil," I told her. I looked at the rococo scrollwork, the lions chasing satyrs chasing maidens chasing cherubs, the cornucopias, the dolphins, the mermaids, and all I could think of was how I'd have to polish it, get it insured, worry about it. How I'd get robbed because I had it. In terms of household goods, what I wanted was a corduroy Happy Baby Carrier.

"I insist," Aunt Lil said, and we were off.

At home, I shoved the epergne in a closet and tried to forget about it. But every time I opened the door, it hissed, "Polish me! Insure me!"

"That epergne is ruining my life," I told my husband. We donated it to the Channel 13 auction.

Six months later Aunt Lil called. She asked how I was enjoying the epergne.

"Oh, I love it." I lied.

"That's funny," she said. "I was watching the Channel Thirteen auction, and they had one just like it there donated by you."

Adrenaline shot to my fingertips. My lips felt carbonated. I was caught in a lie. I made a lame excuse about having two epergnes, and the epergne donated to Channel 13, while similar to hers, was actually the other one. That I needed only one epergne, and hers was so much nicer. I knew she didn't believe it. Who would? I expected her to be angry. I deserved it. Why hadn't it occurred to me that a recluse who collected antiques might be watching the Channel 13 auction? Was there something in Aunt Lil that made me betray her? Was there something in me?

I had made it onto Aunt Lil's hit list. The question was, What took me so long?

I waited for her to hang up on me or say how disappointed she was. But a funny thing happened. She laughed, told me she missed me, and invited us to come up.

"I have an eighteen-karat-gold-mesh etui I've been saving for you," she said. "There's a lapis on the clasp."

I couldn't face someone I'd lied to, even though that meant

hurting her doubly. I hurt her once because I lied to her about the epergne, and then I rehurt her by being too ashamed to face her after lying to her.

Time passed. The phone rang. "I'm not well," Aunt Lil said. "The doctor up here thinks I need an operation."

I did a little research, then made an appointment for her with a gastroenterologist at Columbia-Presbyterian. She hired a driver to take her to the city. I kissed her good-bye as they wheeled her into the OR. After the surgery the doctor found me in the waiting room. His scrub suit was translucent with perspiration. I could see his chest hair through it.

"Your aunt will be fine," the surgeon said. "But I've never had an experience like that. Cutting her large intestine was like sawing through steel."

I suppose that's what happens after eighty-something years of butter and sour cream.

When I visit her the next day, Aunt Lil says, "I'd really like you to come up and take that gold-mesh etui. It's eighteen karat, dear. I got it at an estate sale. A man shot his wife. She'd been keeping company with a poet."

"You keep the etui, Aunt Lil. You enjoy it," I said.

She turned her face to the wall. "I don't understand," she said.

When Aunt Lil left my grandmother's table, the thing the sisters came back to was her long fingernails, how they curved down like talons, how the polish was chipped, how Mandarin they were, how thick, how ridged, and the dirt that collected on their parched and flaky undersides, most likely, I think now, merely residue from spaetzle.

To Cecil —
With sincere
wishes for
a continuation
of our grand
friendship.
Fondly
Audrey

Mom believes you should "never write
anything to a boy you wouldn't want on the
front page of the *New York Times*."

BACON

There are people who say it's impossible to remember events from the age of one. That pre-verbal memories are actually stories you've heard so often, they get codified as memory. But I remember. My sister slams my thumb off in the door. I run to my mother, inter-rupting her phone call in the foyer, and hold it out to show her. And I remember looking up at a light. A black rubber cup like our toilet plunger sinks closer to my face. I wake up in a different crib next to other children in cribs. My mother's face is in the porthole of a swinging door. It disappears, replaced by her friend Ruth's.

Two or more sore throats in a row, and a tonsillectomy was standard operating procedure. It was fun to be sick. There were house calls. Dr. Jackson with his deep, syrupy drawl came into your bedroom and said, "Whale, whale, whale. How's mah little girl?" You had to stay in bed. Sometimes you had to be "tented." You'd sit under a sheet with your head as center pole while a glass vaporizer bubbled and hissed with water and Vicks VapoRub to "break up" your lungs.

"Are you breathing?" My mother listened from outside the tent. "Breathe deep! I don't hear you breathing!"

Recognizable hands slipped food under, a "Spit in the Ocean," Cream of Wheat with sugar and butter, Cream of Rice, cream cheese and olives on rye, tuna on toast, a BLT thick with mayonnaise, fresh orange juice, homemade applesauce, chocolate pudding. Sometimes the hand brought a toy. But the best thing the hand could slide was bacon. You could have bacon every day, and still it was a treat. Our bacon came from the store. It was thickly cut and had a sweet cure on the edges. Usually my mother would have Mattie make the bacon. But on Sunday nights after a long car trip my mother made it. I loved my mother's bacon. She fried it so crispy, the fat waves turned brown.

Every medicine chest had a mysterious black ointment called Ichthyol that came in a sinister tube with a multiperforated nozzle. My sister and I took turns squeezing it out the window, watching the black strings pass out of sight on their way to the pavement. Like everybody, we had Unguentine for burns, Bayer aspirin, a can of Squibb powdered toothpaste, the very strange-smelling witch hazel, Vicks VapoRub for the vaporizer but also for growing pains, a blue-glass eye cup for when something got in your eye and the pharmacist at Whelan's was too busy to take it out, Johnson & Johnson Band-Aids that caused more pain coming off than the injury, Breck shampoo, ipecac (a horrible medicine that made you throw up on the spot and feel better just as fast), and the wonder drug, Desitin. The family dermatological credo was, "If it's wet, dry it. If it's dry, wet it." Desitin worked both ways. It could desiccate a pimple overnight. It could keep scabs moist enough not to fall off prematurely.

Beyond the medicine chest, there was my mother's magic. When a colony of warts popped up on my knee, she rubbed Unguentine in and said, "You may not look at your knee for a week." I didn't. In a week the knee was smooth.

"Warts are psychological," my mother says. "If you believe they'll go away, they will. Before there was Unguentine, your grandmother used hamburger."

"And your warts went away?"

"Of course."

We called all my mother's good friends Aunt. In addition to my real aunts, I had Aunt Hortie (Mom's friend from N.Y.U. she spoke to every morning before getting out of bed), Aunt Dorothy (whose island on Schroon Lake was the high point of summer), Aunt Phyllis (who taught me how to whistle), Aunt Betty (who let me watch her stretch on a Playtex rubber girdle she rolled into a tube), Aunt Honey (who sang on Broadway), Aunt Gladys (Mom's childhood friend from 845 West End Avenue), Aunt Renee (who designed dresses and was married to "Uncle" Harold, the New York City fire commissioner, whose signature was on a sign at Morgen's that read OCCUPANCY BY MORE THAN 194 PEOPLE IS DANGEROUS AND UNLAWFUL), and Aunt Ruth (who owned racehorses and went to the bathroom with the door open so we could keep talking). Most of them aged well. My mother hasn't aged at all. When I tell her this, she tries to prepare me. She waxes pragmatic. If there is any way my mother can bumper life's blows for me, if she could raise her shirt and take each biting, bruising one, she would. So the woman who used to walk backward up Riverside Drive to shield me from the wind says, "I'm not afraid to die. I think of it as a velvet ledge. You're on black velvet, moving along, and then there's nothing there. You slide off the velvet ledge, darling. It's quite comfortable."

Recently she calls to tell me she doesn't want the plots.

At first I think she's saying *plotz*.

"We live in Florida now," she says. "It doesn't make sense to be buried in Westchester. I'm signing them over to you."

"I have to be buried by myself?"

"There are four plots," she says firmly. "You have two. Your cousin Joan has two."

"*Joanie?* I only see her Thanksgiving!"

We laugh. A week later the deed to plot 034, section 24, comes in the mail.

Down in Florida over Christmas, my mother takes me shopping. She's discovered it's easier to drop bombs in the car when she's looking straight ahead.

"You got my letter?" she says, tooling down Palmetto.

"If this is about the plots again, Ma, I don't want the plots. I've decided. I'm getting cremated."

"What?"

I remind her that the last time Dad took me to see his father's grave in Brooklyn, Jacob Volk's stone was listing. The plot was overgrown. Black swastikas were sprayed all over the place, and every piece of glass that protected the photographs on the headstones was smashed. Has she forgotten how Dad's sisters refused to chip in for the upkeep? "I'm going to be cremated, Ma. No one's going to feel guilty because they haven't visited my grave. No one's going to vandalize it. No one's going to fight over the maintenance charges."

"Still," she says, "the thought of it. . . ."

I tell her about my friend Madeline who keeps her mother and father in matching urns in the basement. She waves to them every time she does the wash.

My mother cracks up. What I really want to say is, *You can't die until I can't make you smile.*

Studying the slim, chestnut-haired twenty-year-old in the photo Mom has always kept on her dresser, I ask if Dad still looks like that to her.

"He seems just like the day I met him," she says.

Sitting on his patio, overlooking a lake, my father says, "This isn't a bad last view, is it? This isn't a bad way to go."

"Where ya going?" I say.

Knock wood, ward off the evil eye, I can't picture anything happening to them. They both love their work. They both play killer tennis. They've both had run-ins with scary things, but what does that mean? Most people I know would be dead if it weren't for modern medicine.

"We're not afraid to die," they've told me. "There comes a time when you're ready. We couldn't have imagined that at your age either."

Sometimes I see myself at my father's funeral. Gripping both sides of the lectern, I pause the way Dad would. I develop eye contact. Then I launch into the one about the man who tells his wife he wants his ashes scattered in Bloomingdale's so he can be sure she'll come visit. The idea that something could happen to them won't seem real until it has to. Why should it? What good does it do to taint the present with the inevitable? What good is premature mourning? If you're lucky enough to have healthy parents, do you have to prepare for when your luck runs out?

The elevator door slams. I get the mail. There's a letter from the university I went to asking to be remembered in my will. There's a bulletin from the Authors Guild, they'd like something too. And what's this from Florida?

RE: Florida Statute 765.05—Living Wills
I, Audrey Volk, willfully and voluntarily make known my desire that my dying will not be prolonged under the cir-cumatances [*sic*] set forth below and hereby declare . . .

I consider the misspelling. Is this document valid? I'm sup-posed to let my mother go?

I punch her number. "Ma? I got your present today."

Silence.

"I wanted to get you a Hallmark card. Something appropriate like:

> *Your living will means lots to me.*
> *A gift that suits me to a tee.*

Or maybe:

> *You gave me life!*
> *I help you die!*
> *You're as sweet as*
> *Apple pie!*

We howl. Hurtling toward the apocalypse, we gasp for air.

The next time I go to Florida, they tell me they're going to be buried aboveground in a wall.

"You can go in the horizontal way, or you can go in headfirst. Your father and I have decided to go headfirst."

"Why, Ma?"

"It's cheaper. Less space, darling." Then she adds, "I hope you don't mind. The fellow next to us has a cross."

They are thrilled with the wall. Every time I go to Florida, Dad says, "Want to see the wall?"

Then a year or so goes by, and their dear friend Fran Boxer dies. She's cremated, and they decide they don't want the wall after all. They want to be cremated. My sister is devastated. *The Guide to Jewish Religious Practice* says the Jewish way of burial is "to place the body in the earth." Aboveground burial and cremation are *Nivul Hamet,* "a disgrace to the dead." Some *Nivul Hamets* are arguable. It's *Nivul Hamet* to donate an organ. But it's a *mitzvah* to save a life. Mom and Dad couldn't care less about *Nivul Hamet.* They're agnostics.

Dad tries to sell the slots back to the slot owner, but he refuses to refund the money. "Fine," Dad tells him. "I'll sell them myself."

"You can't," the slot man says. Slot prices are up. The slot man won't be undersold.

Dad writes his congressman. He cc:'s the Attorney General, the local papers, the Better Business Bureau, the Consumer Protection Agency. Dad is energized. He's in full battle mode. He's six feet one and a half of megawatt power. He's right, and he knows it. He owns the slots, hence the slots are his to sell. Dad's latest plan is picketing the slot wall wearing a sandwich board explaining how the slot place violates free trade.

After two months the slot man crumbles. Dad sells the slots for less than the going rate. A couple who wants to go in headfirst gets a bargain. Dad carries a laminated card in his wallet that says who to call to cremate him. He signs up for organ donation and flattens a green bumper sticker onto his car: RECYCLE YOURSELF. BE AN EYE, ORGAN & TISSUE DONOR. He earmarks his new titanium hip for a medical school so they can study the effects of wear. He wants his de-cataracted eyes to go to Columbia's Eye Institute.

Dad tells me his slot victory over the phone. He won't come to New York anymore. He's turned on his birthplace. The last time Dad came up, we spent over an hour in the Museum of Natural History looking for Admiral Peary's sled. In 1909 Admiral Robert Edwin Peary *claimed* he discovered the North Pole. (There's proof that he doctored his journals and so did the explorer Dr. Frederick A. Cook, which means the first man to set foot on the North Pole was someone named Joseph Fletcher, who landed there in an air force C-47 in 1952, but why would I get into that?) Dad used to visit Admiral Peary's sled on Saturday between radiation appointments for acne and the burlesque. I thought I'd known every lonely fact of my father's childhood. I am sad-struck anew thinking about Dad's solitary Saturdays, a twelve-year-old boy with pubescent pimples taking the subway alone to a skin doctor, then going to the burlesque, where for fifty cents he could sit in the balcony and watch the *Earl Carroll Vanities* with "75 of the Most Beautiful Girls in the World."

"I learned to live by myself, for myself," Dad says. "I had no expectations."

We pass the Indian war canoe three times. We scour the basement. All we can find is Roald Amundsen's sled, the one he used crossing the Arctic via the North Pole. That and some threadbare gear from the Antarctic explorer Lincoln Ellsworth. No one can tell us anything about Admiral Peary's sled. None of the guards or information people has *heard* of Admiral Peary.

That does it. Standing outside at the top of the stairs behind J. E. Fraser's statue of Teddy Roosevelt and his guides, staring into the marvelous scrotum of Roosevelt's horse, Dad takes one last look around. "That's it for me," he says. "I've had it with New York."

The fact that Dad won't fly up anymore doesn't stop him from mailing envelopes stuffed with articles:

MUSIC BOOSTS INTELLIGENCE
LAPTOP PROTECTION
TEST YOUR FINANCIAL FITNESS

And just today, MICHELLE PFEIFFER: FORMER OUTCAST.

Sometimes he sends them with a little note: "Thought this would be of service—Dad."

SLIDE WOODEN DRAWERS MORE EASILY
WHAT YOU SHOULD KNOW ABOUT CAFFEINE
BE A WINNER

Four times a year now, Mom comes alone.

"I have a new way of looking at your apartment," she tells me after her latest visit. I'm driving her to La Guardia Airport so she can catch the three-fifty back to West Palm.

"You do, Ma?"

"It's a ruin. It's like visiting the Colosseum or Pompeii."

She's sitting next to me on the front seat. Maybe I should say *folding.* Her body is curved inward, and her head is down so low it's almost touching the seat.

"Ma, why are you sitting like that?"

"It's nothing. I'm a little nervous the way you drive. Really, darling, it's nothing."

The way *I* drive? The last time I was in Boca, Mom drove up on the median three times and kept going left when she meant to go right. "Why are people flashing their lights at us?" she said, ticked until she realized her headlights weren't on.

"When we get to the house," I told her, "I'm going to kiss the driveway."

She gasped. "You think I'm not a good driver?"

M om aims for perfection. Most times she gets a bull's-eye. She'd like to pump some perfection my way too. To that end, she makes lists. The latest one reads:

MOTHER'S LIST

> Reupholster couch
> Take care of IRA
> Fix shelf in Polly's room
> Get round kitchen table and six chairs
> Get large colorful object for coffee table

I have her recipe for "How to Wash Your Face" written in perfect Palmer script:

1. Cleanse with Pond's cold cream
2. Use toner without alcohol, i.e., Nivea, Avon, etc.
3. Night—Orlane Extrait Vitale on first, then Nivea cream
4. Day—Wash with water, use Orlane Extrait Vitale, then Clinique moisturizer. NEVER SOAP.

"You've got to fix that kitchen," she says. "Your daughter will be bringing boys home soon."

Does she mean, Gentlemen callers may one day look at my kitchen and think, How could I marry a girl whose mother has unevenly laid floor tiles and an uninstalled fridge?

Okay, so she's right. The kitchen does need work. Okay, so it looks like a George Booth cartoon. Thanks to a flood upstairs, a cord dangles from the ceiling light fixture and plugs into a wall socket. The broiler hasn't broiled in seven years. That's why we bought the toaster oven, but now that broiler's broken too. ("A simple wiring repair," Dad diagnoses from Florida. "Expose the elements. Clean the contacts. You got a digital multimeter?") My dream fridge arrived three years ago but why install it if I'm planning to redo the countertops and it would have to be taken out again? The inside of the G.E. dishwasher is so rusty I'm calling the internist to see if we need tetanus shots. Yup. Mom's right. The kitchen looks like hell. But do I want my daughter to marry a man who won't marry her because of my kitchen?

Mom stares at my auction find, a portrait of Lord Townley attributed to Romney. (*Attributed to* means *Definitely not done by.*) "You really should have that frame repaired," she says.

Walking into my bedroom: "You still have those lampshades?"

Waiting for the elevator: "Your hair looks so much better today than it did yesterday."

Something snaps. "I have no control over my hair, Ma. It does what it wants to. Every morning I wake up, look in the mirror, and say, 'What the hell?' I never know what's going to stare back at me. I got this hair from you and Daddy. I didn't luck out in the genetic crapshoot. Or maybe they gave you the wrong baby."

"You have *beautiful* hair." Mom looks at me like I'm crack-pated. "Something happened that summer in camp when you cut one side off with manicuring scissors."

Coming out of my bathroom where the tiles from the floor repair were never relaid, she shakes her head. "I don't get it. I don't get it."

What I see as patina, Mom sees as worn. My mother has never owned anything faded. If it's chipped, frayed, or dated, out it goes. She has twenty-eight filled hangers in her closet. If something new comes in, something old gets handed down. Dad cleans her sneakers with bleach on a toothbrush. You could eat off her floors if you don't mind the taste of Pine-Sol.

My apartment needs work. Me too: "If you lose ten pounds, I'll buy you a dress," Ma says.

"You're at an age now where you can't go out without makeup anymore."

"Get a face lift when you're young, before you need it."

Under the fluorescent lights in the supermarket, comparing pretzels, she notices a color anomaly in my hair. "I'm laughing so hard"—she grabs the display—"I think I cracked a rib!"

What she wants for me is an even cleaner, thinner, happier life than she has. Mom made me, and now she will make me better. I'm unfinished, something she can't stop sculpting, something it's her job to complete. It's a sign of her abiding love that she never gives up. It's a sign of my mental health that I never give in. For as long as she's my mother, I am her work in progress. There should be a yellow traffic diamond over my head with the silhouette of a woman with her hands on her hips: DANGER—MOTHER AT WORK.

"You're still wearing that watch?" she says. "You should have a good watch."

I try to explain. "I don't want a good watch, Ma. Someone will steal it. Remember Nana's watch Ilene stole? Remember when you lent me your Lucien Picard for a blind date with Barry Goldwater's nephew, and I left it on the sink at the Playboy Club? Didn't I just lose my watch on a plane? I never want a watch I care about again."

Then we go to the theater. The play is slow. I press a little button on my Timex Indiglo, and it lights up green. "Nineteen ninety-nine at Ames, Ma." I whisper, "You can't do this with a Rolex."

Once, I said, "Ma, don't you ever wonder why I never criticize you?"

She looked shocked. "What could you possibly find to criticize about me?"

Where to start! How to begin! That I think you criticize me too much? I look at her carefully. I am stunned by her expression. She looks like the smartest kid in class, ready to absorb whatever information I can give her and act on it immediately.

"Well"—I think hard—"sometimes in the morning after you

brush your teeth, there's still a little toothpaste on the corner of your lip."

"What? There is? Is there any there now?"

Mom looks in my closet. "You have no clothes," she says, then adds, "Your sister thinks so too."

The next morning my sister calls from Florida. "You have no clothes," she says. "You need more clothes."

What's puzzling is some of the things Mom thinks are wrong, she winds up doing.

"When are you getting carpet?" she asks me. Now she lives in a house with no carpet.

"These windows need drapes," she says. "Aren't you afraid of people looking in?"

Now she lives in a house with no drapes.

"Only Gypsies pierce their ears."

Now she has pierced ears.

As I come out of the shower, my mother asks me if she can fix my hair.

"Sure," I say, and hand her the comb. Then I sit on the bed, like I used to once a week when I was little, on the night she sterilized the combs and brushes with Clorox, and we got our shampoos and she "did" me. It occurs to me that I have never had a Cloroxed comb and brush since then. That I've never Cloroxed for my kids either. Now she's "doing me" again. She's hard at it. The word "gusto" comes to mind as the woman whose hair looks perfect climbing out of a pool attacks mine. I feel like I'm five. It feels good.

She parts my hair, steps back, furrows her brow, studies me, parts it a new way, fluffs the ends with the comb, experiments with bangs, wipes it behind my ears into two letter C's, squints, sets a wave with a chop from the side of her hand, slicks it all back, starts all over, reparts, rechops, refluffs, steps back again.

"See?" She yanks my chin toward the mirror. "It's a look."

Alfalfa stares back at me. Should I tell her that when it dries, it will frizz and go crazy and mash down when I sleep? Doesn't she know that yet? Who on earth knows my hair better than my beloved mother? What can I tell a woman who believes she has the power to alter human follicles with her bare hands? Isn't it time for her to give up?

Never.

So I say, "I get it, Ma. Interesting. Fascinating." And for one minute more, before evaporation starts to take its toll, I am my mother's image of what I should be, what I could be, her love-engorged vision—whatever, God help me, that is.

Mattie Sylvia Lee Myles Weems Watts at my sister's wedding in a Larry Aldrich illusion-top dress. She was my New Year's Eve date for fourteen years.

HASH

Two years before she died, Mattie told me I was her favorite. She had a favorite? Both of us got Mattie's chocolate cake on our birthdays. Both of us played jacks on the kitchen linoleum while she read the sports pages of the *Daily News*. She took us both to the pedodontist, weeping and shredding her hankie while we squirmed in Dr. Adelson's chair. She took us both to the pediatrician too, because my mother was afraid to "take his fire" when we stepped on the scale. Both of us she dressed for school.

Naturally, I tell my sister, "Mattie told me I was her favorite."

"Really?"

"Did you write her from camp?"

"No."

"Did you bring her food?"

"No."

"Did you ever send her a check?"

"I could have been better to Mattie," my sister says.

M attie Sylvia Lee Myles Weems Watts came to live with us when I was one and she was forty-three. "I took one look at how *crisp* Mattie was," my mother says, "and that was it."

Mattie worked every day except Thursday and every other Sunday. She cooked, battled New York soot, and baby-sat. She did everything it takes to run a home except the wash. Wash was done by Lola from Freeport, who was so fat she had to come through the door sideways. Lola rang our back bell, then grunted and wiggled past the jambs while my sister and I angled to watch. The laundry was hand-washed in the pantry sinks, squeezed through a wringer, then pinned to a retractable rack lowered by rope from the kitchen ceiling. Eventually we got a washing machine. But until then Lola did it all by hand, even the sheets.

The rest of the work in our two-bedroom apartment was left to Mattie. Mattie attacked dirt. She stabbed it with her broom. She pummeled it with her dustcloth. She vacuumed carpet till it was raw. "*Now!*" she'd say when something earned her approval, like a perfectly ironed shirt. "*Now!*" She'd stand back admiring the part she'd combed in my hair or roses she'd encouraged with roast beef drippings. "*Now!*" She'd knife the last swath of chocolate icing on her cake, the kind of icing that shatters when you rap it with a spoon. No matter how much we begged, she made it only for birthdays and graduations. The cake never lasted more than a day. Late at night, people bumped into each other groping downstairs for one last sliver. I licked the pot. I sucked the spoons. I scraped the bowl. When the cake was finished, I chewed the doily. This was Mattie's Chocolate Cake, available only for big events.

"Are you going to make the cake?" we'd ask as our birthdays got close. "Promise you'll make the cake?"

"Out of my kitchen." She'd flap her hand.

Mattie was five feet five and so skinny her legs looked like spokes. She wore gold-framed glasses. The tips of her shoes touched when she stood. She had a raised mole in the center of her palm—exactly where my mother had one—that I liked to finger when she held my hand to cross the street. She was a passionate Brooklyn Dodgers fan, although she looked like Satchel Paige, the screwball pitcher for the St. Louis Browns, who said, "If you can't dazzle them with brilliance, baffle them with bullshit." They both had soft faces with full lips and heavy eyebrows. They both looked as if they were holding back a laugh. Mattie's plan was, I'd marry Sandy Koufax, the only Jewish Dodger. She talked about taking me to Ebbets Field, how we'd work our way down to the dugout, and she'd find a way to introduce me, then tell him my good points. I didn't push for it. He was too old. I preferred angry boys who hated their mothers.

Every Thursday, on her day off, Mattie took the subway to Flushing, Queens, to get her hair done. When I first met her, she had braids wound into a crown. As she got older, she blued her hair and wore it in an even roll around her head. Her favorite hairdo was a showstopper—three rows of purple hair snails held rigid in a silver net. She'd sit on a bridge chair while I poked my finger in their perfect coiled centers, row by row, three times around her head. Everything about Mattie said "neat." She was so meticulous, she could train raisins. Half of us hated them, half loved them. Mattie could make a rice pudding in a four-quart bowl and discipline the raisins to stay on the raisin side. She put peas in mashed-potato nests for the sake of beauty alone. She never served bread. Bread was "filler." There was too much other stuff to eat. The exception was Mattie's biscuits. They tanned on the edges and had a texture like dry snow. She made biscuits only when she made fried chicken. We split them steaming, buttered each side to the edge, then covered the melted salt butter with a thick layer of Welch's grape jelly decanted to a crystal jar. (Bottles products came in were verboten on the table.) You could argue that Welch's grape jelly doesn't go with fried chicken. That wasn't the point. We treated the biscuits as an entity unto themselves, the best way to eat a biscuit. We maximized the pleasure of each bite. Old friends who come for dinner still say, "Remember Mattie's steak?" Their eyes glaze. Always I give them the recipe.

MATTIE'S STEAK

Prime Grade-A 14-ounce sirloin
Cross sections of garlic sliced so thin you could
  read the *New York Times* through them
Morgen's seasoning salt
Worcestershire sauce
Peanut oil
A little salt butter

1. Dot the meat on both sides with the garlic.
2. Coat that with Morgen's seasoning salt.
3. Coat that with Worcestershire sauce mixed with a little peanut oil.
4. Turn and baste several times during the day.
5. Sear, then pan-sauté it in a cast-iron skillet rubbed with the butter.
6. Slice at a forty-five-degree angle.

"What's Morgen's seasoning salt?" they ask. Their steaks never come out the same. The last store closed twelve years ago. Except for half a Heinz chili jar of it on my spice shelf, Morgen's seasoning salt no longer exists. Every few years I'll make a steak with my endangered supply, just to keep the taste alive. The closest I can get to a recipe is Dad's vague recollection.

MORGEN'S SEASONING SALT

Salt
Onion salt
Garlic salt
A lot of paprika, to give the steak a good
    brown color

I could have it analyzed by a lab.

Mattie was a perfectionist. She sliced a sandwich on the diagonal, squinting to make sure there was no big half. When she cut leftover roast beef to make hash, each square was the same size. Every quarter-inch cube of beef and potato was browned on six sides. Roast beef was the Sahara of meat, a wasteland of flesh, each mouthful the same except for a paring of crisp garlicky fat crust on the edge. Roast beef was boring. Eating it, a sentence: Twenty bites of hard chewing. The only reason to make roast beef was leftovers for Mattie's hash.

I was five at the height of the New York polio epidemic. No one was sure how you got it. "Never touch a banister!" teachers warned. "Don't wipe your eyes if you wiped your nose first!" "Never swim in a pool!" Kids went to bed fine one night, then woke up unable to move their legs. Our neighbor Susan Brody got it. When we jumped rope in front of the building, Susan sat in her wheelchair with metal braces on her legs and watched. She sang "Fudge, Fudge, Tell the Judge" with us and "I Won't Go to Macy's Any More, More, More." Then a nurse would come down and wheel her upstairs.

"It could be worse," people said. "At least she isn't in an iron lung."

The National Foundation for Infantile Paralysis gave out "Polio Pointers" at school:

DO wash hands carefully before eating and always after using the toilet.
DON'T play with new people.

What we didn't know was that polio was a fecally transmitted disease. Ironically, improved sanitation helped it spread. Indoor plumbing shielded babies from early contact with the virus. When they were exposed to it later, they were more suscepti- ble. The purer water got, the more difficult it was to build up immunity.

Before 1955 and the Salk vaccine, parents panicked. They sent their kids out of the city during the summer, hoping fresh air would protect them. There were cucheleins in the Catskills if you didn't have a lot of money and family compounds by the ocean if you did. And in between, there were sleep-away camps in piney places. Public school ended on June 30, and that night Grand Central Terminal teemed with kids in camp caps and regulation shorts clutching turkey sandwiches and the newest Archie comics. Camp Red Wing met under the west balcony on the north side. The air was filled with the screams of girls who hadn't seen their camp best friend in ten months. We'd board the sleeper in hot Manhattan, and when we opened our eyes, we were in the Adirondacks. Parents, who might have been exposed to polio in the city, were forbidden to kiss or touch us when they came up for visiting day.

Sleep-away camp was fine with me, but only if Mattie mailed her hash. I didn't want to live two months without it. I took a stand. Mom said it was impossible to mail hash.

"Keep my thermos and mail it in that," I said. Then I got to camp and loved the food. Willie and Frances, married French chefs from the city, made Poulet au Sauce Supreme, Boeuf en Daube, and Fried Fillet of Sole with capers, tarragon, and sieved egg in the Sauce Tartare. Toast was brushed with clarified butter, then baked in the oven. Royal icing dotted the Galettes Sablées. On visiting days my father would make a formal inspection of the camp kitchen, endearing himself to Willie and Frances, who then gave me extra marzipan roses on my birthday cake—the ultimate bargaining power at Camp Red Wing.

Watching Mattie, I learned the two most important rules of cooking: Patience and Clean as You Go. I also learned that because of my place in our family, I got a full-size bathtub while she got a New York maid's-room half. I got a big bedroom, while hers was smaller than my mother's dressing room. The leitmotif of childhood was an ever-burning fury that I had more than Mattie. Accompanying Mom to Ohrbach's for a new handbag, I grieved to see it cost twenty dollars more than Mattie made a week. Mothers talked about salaries while they sat on the benches in the playground. They kept on eye on their kids in the sandbox and an eye on the mother who might pay a housekeeper more than the going rate. It was made clear that if you got a new housekeeper, you would pay what everybody else was paying or less. That way, no beloved housekeeper would leave you for a better-paying job. It was salary-fixing. A common refrain was, "Don't ruin it for us."

I was crazed by the injustice. If Mattie made forty-five dollars a week and she worked five and a half days and she got up at seven and went to bed at eleven, that was fifty-one cents an hour, and when she took the subway to Queens, it was a quarter each way, which meant she had to work an hour just to make enough money to get to and from the beauty parlor. If she bought me peanuts from the machine in the subway, that was ten cents, eleven minutes of hard labor. My mother said Mattie *chose* to wait in the car on road trips when we ate at Howard Johnson's. When Mattie asked for one Saturday night off a month so she could see her "steady fellow," my mother, who went out Saturday nights, said, "That would be quite impossible." The rare times Mattie had a visitor, he came up the back elevator, entered through the back door where the garbage was, and went directly to her dark room.

M attie had two kinds of breakfasts: leftovers, and when there weren't any leftovers, Velveeta on a teaspoon dunked in coffee with cream and sugar. She'd sit on a stool with her back against the heating pipes sucking the warm softened cheese. Mattie sailed even-tempered and steady the eighteen years she took care of me. When I was banished from the dinner table and sent to my room, Mattie smuggled in a plate. The time she caught me in bed with a boy, she got a broom and chased him out of the house. She loathed Harry after that. But it was his fault for getting into bed with me, not mine for raising the covers.

Once I made her cry. My parents were on vacation. I hated my coordinated all-pink room with the butterfly wallpaper and matching butterfly spreads. I pulled out the carpet and pried up the tacks. I stripped off the wallpaper, lacquered my faux French bureau white, unscrewed the shutters, and sprayed the headboards black. I took the Long Island Railroad into New York and bought my first desk and talked my grandmother into a pair of army-green bedspreads from Altman's.

"Oh, no." Mattie sniffled from the doorway. "Oh, no. Your mother's gonna *murder* me." But she didn't try to stop me, and I knew she would defend me. Mattie was on my side. She was the youngest in her family too. "We're the underdogs," she liked to say. She thought it was shameful we wore hand-me-downs. I liked hand-me-downs. I liked clothes with a past. I didn't like to look primped. Maybe because I couldn't look primped. The back of my socks wound up under my arches. My hair was berserk. I wanted to move the easy way boys moved. I wanted to bounce and jangle when I walked and not worry about clothes. Pinching my cheeks with rouge on her fingers before I left for a party, my mother would say, "Now don't be loud!" I wanted to be whatever I was. Was I loud? If I was loud, what was wrong with loud? Hand-me-downs were fine with me. Less to worry about, and weren't two used blouses better than one new one?

The summer I turned nine Mattie left for her birth-place, Rome, Georgia, where she said the best peaches in the world came from. While she was gone, my mother was thrown from a horse in Central Park. Dad carried her to the Ninety-sixth Street transverse and flagged down a car. Her back was broken. The choice was surgery or lying flat for six weeks. Mom chose flat. She called Mattie to see if Mattie would cut her vacation short and come up. But Mattie had decided to retire. She was going to get false teeth. Why couldn't she get false teeth in New York?

At least once a day my sister and I saw her walking toward us down the street.

"Look! There's Mattie!" and we'd both start running. Then we'd get closer, and it wasn't Mattie.

In Mattie's place Mom rehired Anna Offerman, who'd been my grandmother's housekeeper when Mom was growing up. Anna had a heavy German accent, a frizzy white perm, and smelled like old onions. My sister used to fire her twice a day. She called us "Jackass."

"You Yock-oz." She'd trudge into our bedroom, brandishing her gray mop like a Valkyrie. "You leef in a peeg-sty!"

I wrote Mattie begging her to come back. "Anna Offerman is poisoning me! HELP!" We tried to make Anna quit by placing scissors on the sofa just before she plopped down. We refused to let her watch Liberace. Anna would turn the dial to the Liberace channel, then slump on the couch with her rough red hands folded on top of her belly. Then my sister and I would take turns jumping up to flip the station. Anna would lurch herself and flip it back. Eventually she'd give up. "Ach! You boat Yock-oz!" If we made Anna miserable enough, we reasoned Mattie would come back to us.

When I was eleven, I left our New York apartment for camp, and when I came home, it was to a new place in the suburbs. As I reached for the knob, the door swung open from inside. And there she was, Mattie! I hurled myself into her. I hugged her and sucked in her smell, part almond from Jergen's lotion, part bergamot. I buried my face in the bright white perfection of her uniform. She laughed and patted me. A door opens, and the thing you want most in the world is there. This happened more than forty years ago. I can still feel it—the moment I got the thing I thought I could never have.

We never mentioned race. Discussing race would have been "in bad taste." The words "Negro," "segregation," and, God forbid, "colored" were stricken from our vocabulary. "Africa" and "servant" were taboo too. If a guest said "black" within hearing range of Mattie, as in "Churchill called his depression 'the black dog,' " we froze. Our eyes darted wildly until someone changed the subject. If a guest called a housekeeper "maid" or "the girl," that guest was not invited back. It was a bizarre New York Jewish sensibility that we could somehow protect Mattie from prejudice by never acknowledging there was such a thing as color in the first place. We pretended to be color-blind, and yet my mother rang for Mattie with a crystal bell. Mattie wore a uniform. I'd study her face when Mom jingled her to clear. Mattie did not appear to mind. But I did. I minded big-time. My mother would not like to be rung for. How dare she ring for Mattie?

Three years ago a national magazine asked me to write an essay on someone who'd been important to me. I chose Mattie. The editor phoned after reading the piece.

"We love it!" she said. "I just have a couple of changes. Could you remove the reference to C.O.R.E.? Could you take out her other names and just call her Mattie? Could you delete her birthplace and that bit about giving her a subscription to *Ebony* for Christmas?"

"Why?"

"Our readers don't want to know she's black."

Mattie and I spent fourteen New Year's Eves together. She was my steady Saturday night date too. Our ritual was Swanson's TV Turkey Dinners at the bridge table while watching *Route 66, 77 Sunset Strip*, then *Gunsmoke*. I learned about interactive TV from Mattie. "Watch out, Mr. Dillon!" she'd scream. And "Hurry, Chester! He's got a *gun*!" We threw pillows at the set. That's why they were called throw pillows. We believed we could influence the outcome. Because of our intimate relationship with the television, I waited for Mel Torme to call me at home. After school he had a show called *Mel Torme and the Mel-Tones*. I loved Mel Torme. He was beautiful but not so beautiful he couldn't fall in love with me. I wrote our phone number on one of my father's shirt cardboards and held it up to the TV. Every day while Mel Torme sang, I'd sit in front of the TV holding up "SC.4-3290." When Mel didn't call, it broke my heart until I realized the numbers probably looked like mirror-writing to Mel through the screen and he couldn't read them.

Until I left for college, Mattie woke me for school the same way every day. "Get up!" she'd holler at the foot of the stairs, and when I didn't, she'd drop a cold, wet washcloth on my face and laugh. Then I'd sit down to her idea of a balanced breakfast: two eggs sunnyside up, six rashers of crisply fried bacon, two pieces of buttered toast, a four-ounce glass of freshly squeezed orange juice, and an eight-ounce glass of milk. In the kitchen, she'd be eating Velveeta or leftovers, congealed spaghetti, chicken necks.

"Why are you eating that for breakfast?" I'd ask.

"My stomach doesn't know what time it is," she'd say, or "You think fish and onions and cream are any better?"—a slur on pickled herring.

Then she'd send me off to school with a ham and Swiss, carrot and celery sticks, fruit, and cookies. When I was sick, she cooked "Spit in the Ocean," an egg fried in a circle cut out of a piece of white bread, a.k.a. "Toad in the Hole." She introduced me to the wonder of peanut butter and mayonnaise on rye. She didn't rat when I palmed string beans and brussels sprouts down my underpants to flush away later.

When Mattie turned seventy-five, she retired again. This time she didn't want to, but Mom was ready for an invisible housekeeper, the kind that speaks a foreign language and doesn't expect conversation. Mattie found an apartment on Edgecombe Avenue in her best friend Nita's building. The place was so small the bed touched three walls. Then she got another job, cooking for a Mr. Ollendorf of the Ollendorf Art Moving Company. I'd gone to college with his grandson, Tommy Ollendorf, a smart, well-mannered guy, and wasn't surprised when Mattie told me she liked Mr. Ollendorf. He was lucky to get her thoughtful care.

When Mattie's legs gave out and she couldn't climb two flights of subway stairs twice a day, she retired permanently. Her days were spent following the sun on the benches of Morningside Heights. Mattie always knew where to go for warmth. I'd send money and bring food. She liked tuna, bananas, and bourbon. We'd call each other. She would tell me her dreams. In one of them she saw me give birth "to a big, screaming boy-child." Nine months later Peter, weighing 8 pounds 12 ounces, was born.

Mattie died in the bathtub. She was eighty-two. Nita, whom she calls Bonehead, phones to tell me. I've known Nita for years, and we make a date to meet. She gives me two black dolls that belonged to Mattie. Chi-Chi and Carmen are dressed like Carmen Miranda, with gold hoops in their ears and fruit on their heads. Nita gives me a patchwork quilt Mattie made too. I used to sit next to Mattie on her bed and watch her piece a quilt. She'd have two brown paper bags: One was greasy and full of Spanish subway peanuts she liked to flick in my mouth. The other bag was stuffed with triangles of cloth she'd pull out and squint at. She had the habit of adjusting her glasses by wiggling her nose.

I am holding a quilt Mattie made. The batting is coming out in five places. There are rips and open seams. It doesn't matter. I take it to Camille Dalphond Cognac, founder of the Quilt Restoration Society in Hillsdale, New York.

"Can you fix this?" I ask.

She unfolds the quilt on a large table. She gasps.

"Sometimes in this business you think you've seen everything," she says. "And then you see a quilt like this."

"What do you mean?"

She thinks for a moment. "Whoever made this was obviously very happy."

"You can tell that?"

"It has joy all over it."

"What else can you tell?"

"There's a folk-art element. It's a variation on Grandmother's Flower Garden—three hexagons, added leaves plumbed on a square. The fabrics are late thirties and forties. It was made from the scraps of the scraps, housedresses, pajamas. Look"—she points to a place where an edge is cleverly stitched to compensate for a crooked piece next to it—"it doesn't line up. It's called 'Make it fit.' "

"I'm surprised," I say. "The woman who made this was a perfectionist."

"For pleasure," Camille says, "we do what we would not do in the front parlor."

I ask Camille how much Mattie's quilt will cost to fix.

"There are multiple-task activities on this quilt," she says. "It'll cost about two hundred dollars. But," she adds, "if you want a quilting lesson, I could teach you how to fix it yourself for fifteen dollars, and you'll be prepared for any quilt emergency."

"You can teach me how to fix it?"

"I can teach a Mack truck driver in under an hour."

A few months later I come back with the quilt. Camille reexamines it. "I have a quiet understanding of what's going on here."

Camille threads a needle. She observes my running stitch and backstitch and shows me how to improve them. She teaches me the ladder stitch. "It becomes invisible." When by mistake I sew a piece on inside out, she says, "I give absolution for terrible things." We spend the day together sewing and talking and laughing, and I tell her about Mattie and she tells me about her sons and I think, How wonderful quilting bees must have been, women coming together and making something beautiful and useful, that particular flow of conversation that happens when your hands and eyes are mindfully engaged.

I sew through Mattie's needle holes, replace some batting. It feels like spending time with Mattie again. Camille gets out a clear plastic bag. Carefully she folds the quilt.

"Can I come back if I run into trouble?"

"You'll be all right," she says.

"I will?"

"When in doubt, follow Mattie."

I have only three photos of Mattie. When you pointed a camera at her, she put her hand in front of her face. One shows Mattie clapping at my sister's wedding. One was shot on the beach at Brill Island—Aunt Dorothy's place on Schroon Lake—where Mattie liked to fish for sunnies. In the third photo Mattie is five. Three neat children surround their long-necked mother in her black floor-length dress. Everyone looks serious except for Mattie, who looks sad. She'd begged her mother to comb her hair grown-up style before the picture was taken, and her mother had refused. The photo was taken right before Mattie's father died. When I asked her about her child-hood, she replayed the same stories each time: How she cried when her mother did her hair before the picture. How, when walking along the top of a fence after she'd been forbidden to, she fell headfirst into a steaming heap of dung. How she couldn't eat duck, because she'd had to kill them. How her preacher step-father had sent her to church with the family picnic and somehow during the service her hand kept creeping under the lid and picked all the fry off the fried chicken and all the icing off the cake. How her mother died when she was ten, and she went to live with her grandfather in Riverdale, Georgia. How he sent Mattie to work in the post office and kept her salary, so she ran away to Atlanta with a girlfriend. How she married cruel men. How she never had children. "God just didn't mean for some people to have them." Then she'd laugh and say, "You're my child! *Now!*"

I don't know if Mattie and I ever talked about anything more profound than how to get bubbles out of cake batter once it's poured into a tin or not to use Brillo on Formica. I wish we had. Regardless, she's with me. I have three recurrent dreams. Two are bad: First, I am losing my teeth in a social situation and have to spit them out like watermelon seeds to keep from choking. Second, I go back to college, but no one knows me and there's no place to live and my old boyfriend I was horrible to couldn't care less. My third recurrent dream is good: It's about a door. I am in a room, and suddenly there's a door I've never seen before. I open it and something wonderful I couldn't have imagined is on the other side. Sometimes it's the Garden of Eden. Or an extra bedroom. Once it was a waterfall. When it happened in real life, it was Mattie. The four letters and birthday card I have from her I keep in my bureau tied with a red ribbon. "Dear Patty," one goes. "Just a note to say hello and that I am doing fine. It's still very warm here how is it there? How are you doing in school good I hope. Have you cleaned up your room yet I know you have not. I miss you very much. Hope to see you soon. What your new boyfriend's name. Thank you for your letters. Thank your mother for the lovely card. Tell her I am doing fine. I will have my teeth before Christmas. Please write me soon. Love, Mattie."

MATTIE'S CHOCOLATE* CAKE

2 sticks butter, at room temperature
½ box powdered sugar, sifted
3 eggs
2 capfuls vanilla extract
1½ cups flour, measured AFTER sifting
1 teaspoon baking soda

1. Preheat oven to 350°F.
2. Grease an 8-inch tube pan 4 inches high with butter and dust with flour.
3. Fluff butter with a rotary beater GOING ONLY IN ONE DIRECTION THE WHOLE TIME.
4. Add powdered sugar a little at a time to the butter.
5. Add eggs, one at a time.
6. Add vanilla.
7. Add flour mixed with baking soda.

Spatula the mix into the tube pan, smooth it, and bounce the pan against the counter until the batter is level. DO NOT OPEN OVEN DOOR TO CHECK CAKE FOR FIRST HALF HOUR. Then stab every ten minutes with the paper end of a match till it comes out clean.

*This is a yellow cake. But since it exists solely as a place to hang Mattie's Chocolate Icing, we call it Mattie's Chocolate Cake.

MATTIE'S CHOCOLATE ICING

1½ cups granulated sugar
1 cup water
2 double squares unsweetened chocolate
¾ stick butter, room temperature
2 capfuls vanilla extract

1. Mix sugar and water together over high heat in covered pot. Boil until syrup strings.
2. Melt chocolate without direct heat.
3. Stir chocolate into sugar, and turn down heat for 3 minutes. Stir the whole time.
4. When mixture turns gray, stir in butter.
5. Add vanilla and BEAT WITH SPOON.
6. Add a little milk or more butter if it looks too thick.
7. Knife icing onto cake.

In *The New Yorker* E. B. White called Jacob
Volk "the greatest wrecker of all time."

On the job demolishing the old Princeton College plot in New Jersey, Jacob Volk walked into his bank and noticed a teller with chestnut hair. My father's father was forty-two when they married. She was seventeen. He had the underwear for Ethel Edythe Shure's trousseau tatted by nuns in Switzerland. On their wedding day, mindful of the Orthodox tradition, he did not forget the poorest of the poor, making donations to the Daughters of Jacob, the Rabbi Jacob Joseph School, Machsikei Talmud Torah, Hebrew Day Nursery, Keidaner Association Charity Fund, Tipheret Israel, the Bronx Hospital, and the New York Federation of Charities.

Jake leveled the lot in Bensonhurst he'd won in a card game from Mayor James J. "Jimmy" Walker and built his bride a house. He designed a marble shower with eighteen silver heads that pelted everything on three sides from the ankles on up, and a frieze of Volk family crests that girdled the second floor. He took Ethel on a grand tour and bought her monogrammed place plates from Czechoslovakia, challah knives from Holland, and a dancing-girl piano lamp with a liftable skirt from Bohemia. My son, Peter, shaves with the fitted kit Jake picked up in London.

"Is he oiling the leather?" Dad asks now and then.

When they returned from their honeymoon, Jake gave her a Stromberg-Carlsson "Marconi." Evenings they'd turn it on, and Jake would open the living-room windows so the neighbors could sit on their orange crates in his garden and listen.

Jake's father, Sussman Volk, left Lithuania for New York in 1887. He'd been a miller in Vilna, but New York was already a big city and didn't need millers. Sussman had seven children. He took stock of what he could do and became a tinker. He sold pots and pans off his back. On the road he slept in the stables of the people he sold pots to. While praying one morning, Sussman was kicked by a horse which made him tear his hair and shout, "My life lacks dignity!"

Once again Reb Sussel changed careers. Being a religious man, he knew how to butcher meat. He opened a small butcher shop at 86½ Delancey Street. The first week, a Romanian friend stopped by.

"Could you store a trunk for me in the basement?" he asked. "I've got to go back to Romania for a few years."

"If I store your trunk," Reb Sussel said, "what will you give me?"

"If you store my trunk, I will give you the recipe for pastrami."

Sussman took the trunk and the recipe and began selling hunks of pastrami over the counter. Customers liked it so much, they started dropping by for a slice. Then they wanted the slices between two pieces of rye. Before long they were coming in for sandwiches more than they were coming in for meat. Sussman Volk brought pastrami to the New World. He moved from 86½ Delancey Street to 88 Delancey Street, put in a few tables, and the first New York deli was born. Legend has it that about this time his older brother, Uncle Albert, became the first man to stir scallions into cream cheese.

Sussman and Sarah had four daughters and three sons. The

girls—Becky, Hannah, Anna, and Ettie—couldn't agree on anything. When they met for lunch, they each went home a different way. Albert, Leonard, and my grandfather were the boys. Every day after school all seven of the children worked in the deli making toodles. A toodle is a little square of waxed paper rolled into a cone with a dollop of mustard in it. You could take a toodle to work in the morning with a piece of cold meat and squeeze a squiggle of fresh mustard on it at lunch. But Jake didn't like making toodles. He didn't like being told what to do. So he quit the deli and got a job taking tickets on the Fifth Avenue trolley. On his first run he bumped into a woman he knew. "You, Jake? A conductor?" she said. He rode to the end of the line and got off. But not before he noticed a building being taken down. He scraped together three hundred dollars and bought a horse and wagon, crowbars, and sledges. On the side of the wagon he painted what became his lifetime logo: "The Most Destructive Force on Wall Street."

At first, the lone New York Jew in shoring and wrecking had trouble finding work. Then he got an idea. He'd do something nobody else did. He'd offer to pay for the privilege of tearing buildings down. He'd make his profit salvaging mantelpieces, doors, wood panels, chandeliers, conduits, steel, pipe, and scrap iron. He'd bundle and recycle the wood.

Jake got busy. Everything he demolished was sold. Broken bricks and concrete that weren't salvageable got dumped in New York swamps for landfill. Unemployed men called Klondikers chipped cement off good bricks, and Jake got a nickel for each one. Like his father-in-law, who had a junkyard in Princeton, and his son, who makes sculptures out of Dumpster finds, Jake knew everything had worth. He paid his men on Friday in his offices at 103 Park Avenue. He paid them in cash, then offered them a swig from a bottle of whiskey he kept on his desk next to a blackjack.

Two years before she met William Randolph Hearst, Marian Davies had an affair with Jake. He liked women. She liked powerful, heavy-jawed men. But starting out, Jake couldn't afford to live on his own. He asked his older brother, Albert, if it would be okay to move in with him. "You can stay at my place on one condition," Albert said. *"No women."*

Then Albert came home early one afternoon and found a pink feather floating in the air above his bed.

"Out!" He pointed to the door.

Wrecking was a gambler's game. Contracts contained time clauses. A wrecker had to pit his experience against the strength of walls. Jake had gone to technical schools on the Lower East Side. He understood the value of speed. He used this understanding to invent a faster way to gut a building. He called it the Upside-down Method of House Wrecking. During the first quarter of the century, there were all kinds of buildings in New York: skeleton-frame, wall-bearing types, fireproof buildings made of steel and concrete. Using the Upside-down Method, Jake attacked them inside from the first floor instead of the top. He left only enough of the structural frame to support the walls. As the demolition continued, the debris fell inward, accumulating at the bottom of the building's shell. Shovels moved in. Jake carried a stopwatch. He timed it. Power shovels could fill a seven-yard truck in three minutes. The same amount of debris took a half hour to load using chutes from the top of a building connected to hoppers. Jake tore down the Cotton Exchange so fast he got a bonus of thirty thousand dollars. In his *New Yorker* obituary, E. B. White said Jake had "a genius for speed." He toppled the Third Avenue El to make way for the subway. He tore down banks so that bigger banks could rise. After Jake died, his brother Albert used the Upside-down Method to clear three midtown blocks for the construction of Rockefeller Center. Two hundred buildings were demolished.

A round the time of the Upside-down Method, Jake got another idea. Ramming had been used for razing since Mesopotamia. But ramming wasn't effective on New York's multistoried buildings. How do you ram a skyscraper? On the other hand, what if you could ram *in the air*?

What if you could attach something to a crane and what you attached did the ramming? What if the thing that rammed was on a chain that swung so the rammer could build momentum? The wrecking ball was born.

Jake took down the old Bankers Trust Building at the corner of Nassau and Wall Streets, directing a hundred men from the ground with a megaphone. According to *Distinguished Jews of America,* although the work was dangerous, "one of the great characteristics of Mr. Jacob Volk is that he never sends a man where he would not go himself."

Jake loved every part of taking down a building, from laying the plans to selling the mantels. In thirty years he demolished twenty-five hundred buildings. That's eighty-three buildings a year, or one and three-quarters a week. Jake hated the buildings of Stanford White. They were made too well. "When he built 'em, they stayed built," Jake said. Normally when his men chopped a hole in a floor ten percent the size of the floor, the other ninety percent caved in. Not in a White building. The firm of McKim, Mead & White (hundreds of whose landmarked buildings still stand) patented a vaulting system that used four-inch by eight-inch Guastavino tiles. Between two layers of these tiles was a layer of concrete. A White floor was self-supporting. If you made a hole in a White floor ten percent the size of the floor, you'd have to make nine more holes.

Is this something only a demolitionist's family fantasizes about? I like to pretend I have the power to knock down any three buildings in New York. Most of the time, it's the same three buildings, the three that bring me up short every day: 40 East Ninety-fourth Street, a faceted beige-brick behemoth with bronze windows completely out of scale and character with my neighborhood. And 45 East Eighty-ninth Street, an Emery Roth & Sons tower with a scooped-out façade that creates a punishing wind tunnel whenever there's a breeze. And the MetLife building behind the Helmsley Building. The Helmsley Building didn't need a backdrop. Looking south, the silhouette of the Helmsley Building (originally the New York Central Building) was an instant blast of neo-Baroque light-shaped beauty and a salute, with its giant gilded God-flanked clock, to the glory and precision of America's railroads. The MetLife Building (still called the Pam Am building) turned a fifty-one-block vista into a dead end. I'd be happy reducing it to rubble.

In keeping with tradition, Jake and his sisters all named their firstborn sons after their father, Sussman Volk. My father is Sussman Volk too, and his three first cousins are Sussman Stavin, Sussman Fleschner, and Sussman Joseph. The four boys were nicknamed Sussel, which became Cecil. Cecil Volk, Cecil Stavin, Cecil Fleschner, and Cecil Joseph. They never changed their names legally, but that's what it says on their passports.

When Jake died, he left an estate worth $254,000. Finally his sisters agreed on something. They wanted that money. Ettie, Becky, Hannah, and Anna got together and sued to take Jake's children from their mother. They said Ethel couldn't manage money. That she'd squander the children's annuities. The sisters were right. Ethel didn't know the first thing about money. When she wanted something, "No" wasn't an option. If she passed a store with something pretty in the window, she'd stop in the street, take out her address book, and see who she could send it to.

Eventually Ethel won the lawsuit. She kept her three children then gave two away. The eldest, Aunt Helen, was raised by Ethel's parents in Princeton. And even though Jake wanted my father to be a rabbi, Dad was plucked out of Yeshiva and shipped off to military school so he could "learn to be a man." At twenty-nine, Ethel was a rich and beautiful widow encumbered by only one little girl.

Jake's executors made sure his wishes were honored. My grandmother couldn't remarry before all three children married, or she'd forfeit her trust. The will also specified that the children could not get the balance of their trusts until they married. If a child married out of the faith, that child would forfeit his or her inheritance to be divided among the other children. It was a will that encouraged Jacob's progeny to find someone Jewish, fast. Aunt Helen fell in love with a Catholic named Vance, but she married a Jew. Aunt Harriet dropped out of high school and married four days after she turned eighteen. When my father married at twenty, he was Ethel's last child to wed. That's what she was waiting for. Seven days later she married her boyfriend, Charles Wolf. The name Volk means people, or folk, in German. But in Russian, Volk means wolf. Ethel Volk Volk. Ethel Wolf Wolf. Ethel Volk Wolf. Ethel Wolf Volk.

Jake was no stranger to control-from-the-grave wills. Reb Sussel's was a tontine, a system of money dispersal introduced by a Neapolitan banker named Lorenzo Tonti to France in the seventeenth century. In a tontine money is shared equally among a group of people, but as each person dies, what's left of his or her share is divided among the survivors. When Sussman died, he left equal shares in the deli to his six remaining children. But as each Volk child died, they could not leave their shares to their own families. Their shares reverted to their siblings. I don't know who Reb Sussel's last surviving child was. But a few years ago I wrote an essay that mentioned the deli, and the phone rang. A woman I'd never heard of introduced herself. "I'm Cecil Joseph's daughter," she said.

"Oh!" I said. "You must be Annie Volk Joseph's granddaughter!"

We talked for a few minutes about the family. Then she said, "Listen. You know the key money from the deli? It's still in escrow, but my father's mother was the last remaining child from that generation, so I hope you're not going to give me a hard time about it."

"You're kidding," I said.

"No," she said.

"How much?" I asked.

Softly she hung up the phone.

My grandmother tried to run the Jacob Volk Wrecking and Shoring Company herself. It went under fast. Meanwhile, Jake's brother prospered with the Albert A. Volk House Wrecking & Excavating Company and the Albert A. Volk Building Materials Corporation. In his spare time, Albert A. (for Abba) wrote letters to the *New York Times* about Churchill and Roosevelt, letters urging the amendment of the Wagner Act, increased tree planting on city streets, prolonged war on Germany, and fear of black cats. The *Times* published dozens of letters. Then they published the rebuttals. Then they published Albert's rebuttals to the rebuttals. Heated letters went back and forth. Eventually a *Times* reporter knocked on Albert's door.

HERE'S ONE READER WHO LIKES WRITING—ALBERT VOLK'S LETTERS TO EDITORS ON PROBLEMS OF THE DAY ARE HIS MAIN PLEASURE, the headline read.

"You think I'm a crackpot?" Albert asked the reporter. "Well, maybe I am. But what is a crackpot? It is anyone who is cracked about different things than you are cracked on."

The interview appeared on October 4, 1948, but part of my copy has been excised. I go to the microfilm room at the New York Public Library. Someone in the family has neatly removed the following: "He was ousted from two public schools and finally quit the third at the age of 13 to work for a hymn writer. Five weeks later he was discharged for suggesting a rhyme to go with 'Jesus with faltering feet.'" The interview ends with Albert's saying, "I can't help laughing to myself. Me and my silk hat. I came here in steerage and I have attained Fifth Avenue. I get a big laugh out of that."

When it came time for my father to work, Dad asked Albert for a job. Albert took him on as a night watchman. From eleven p.m. to seven a.m. Dad paced deserted lots with a German shepherd until it occurred to him that Albert A. Volk had no desire to see his brother's son flourish. Albert married the governor of Puerto Rico's daughter but never had children. On his deathbed he hooked his finger, signaling the family to move closer. Dad was there. He likes to use the creaky voice of an old, toothless man when he quotes Albert's last words: "I want you to promise me you'll read my will as my coffin is being lowered into the grave. I want everyone to know exactly what they're crying about."

My father has few memories of his father. When he was learning to walk, Jake would take his hand and sing, "One, two, three! Walk with me!" My father says Jake kept a cat-o'-nine-tails on the back of the kitchen door and used it on him. "I noodled with the nails that held it together," Dad says. "I helped it to fall apart." Jake never hit his daughters, but when my grandmother stood between Dad and the cat, sometimes she got hit.

"You beat your son then," Dad says. "It was supposed to be good for him."

The worst beating Jake ever gave my father was when he caught Dad playing stickball on Rosh Hashanah.

"He was good with a belt too," Dad says. "He could whip it off fast."

A cat-o'-nine-tails is a round wooden baton with nine tails of leather or cord nailed to it. Each tail is two feet long and has three knots at two-inch intervals, the first knot being two inches from the end. When the tails land on a back, their spread is never more than three inches. A three-quarter-inch-thick plank of pine flies apart when flogged once with a cat-o'-nine. In the hands of an eager bosun's mate, naval flogging, which was suspended in 1871, easily killed.

What kind of man flogs his little boy?

Where did Jake find an instrument of torture that was outlawed before he was born?

Was it part of Jake's genius for speed to persuade by force?

What kind of man was he?

According to Granny's sister Rose, "Jake would yank Ethel by the hair if she looked at another man."

"What do you mean?" I ask.

"Once, in the car, we pulled alongside another car, and Ethel smiled at the driver," Aunt Rose says. "Jake jerked her head around by the hair."

"He was affectionate and generous," Aunt Eva, the youngest sister, counters. "We looked forward to his visits in Princeton. He bought lavish gifts. Every piece of furniture we had came from him. He bought us our first radio."

Jake used to introduce his children as "My Three Diamonds," and wear a pinkie ring with three diamonds in it. He cleaned his nails with a gold pocketknife I now keep on my key ring. I use his Waltham watch and store my pencils in his kneeling Indian tobacco jar. Every day my hands touch things his hands touched. In our living room there's a framed poster with one hundred and ten photos on it titled "Notables of Greater New York." The portraits are of people who contributed to the creation of the New York Municipal Building, "the largest structure undertaken at that time by any municipality." If you laid its forty-one floors side by side, a farm of twenty-seven acres would be completely covered. The building was designed by McKim, Mead & White and built by the Thompson-Starrett Company. Whenever I have jury duty, I stroll the colonnade and think, My grandfather cleared the land for this. Jake's picture is on the poster along with J. P. Morgan's, Elsie de Wolfe's, Andrew Carnegie's, and Madame Pacquin's of hand-cream fame. My eye goes straight to Jake, though, third row down, third from the left, starched white collar, stony eyes, the possibility of a smile.

Jake never took my father to a fight or a game, but he did introduce him to the Russian Baths on Second Avenue, where the tougher you were, the higher you sat, because heat rises. Afterward, an old Russian beat Dad with maple leaves. Once, Jake came home with a puppy in each pocket. My father liked to come home with surprise pets too: Cookie Lulubelle, a manic foxhound he picked up at a firehouse. Morgen, a male beagle I had a pretty good relationship with until somebody explained what he was doing to my calf wasn't hugging. Tabby, a gift-wrapped cat under our Christmas tree, who routed my forearm. We celebrated Christmas, not Chanukah, despite Dad's Orthodox origins. We were nonobservant Jews, assimilated anti-Roosevelt lefties. Restaurateurs blamed Roosevelt for the unions. You couldn't fire a waiter unless he was caught red-handed gambling or stealing. A waiter could come in soused, smelling like the bottom of a shoe, he could snarl at a customer, and you couldn't fire him. We were quasi-liberals terrified of signing a petition, because petitions leave records that could haunt you. My father didn't vote. He was in the store before the booths opened. When the League of Women Voters called every year, I would hear him say, "Madam, I'm terribly sorry. I can't vote. I'm a Danish Nationalist."

In 1929 Harold Ross asked Robert Coates to write a profile on Jake for *The New Yorker.* Jake died before it had a chance to run. Ross didn't run profiles on dead people, so James Thurber assigned E. B. White to write something shorter. White laid Jake to rest in "Talk of the Town." I wrote to Astrid Peters Coates asking if she knew where I might find a draft of her husband's piece. She wrote back saying Coates's papers were in the Special Collections of the University of Wyoming. I made contact on the Internet. A librarian e-mailed me back: "I have researched the Robert Coates Papers (7144) but I am sorry to report that there are no references or records about Jacob Volk." Maybe Coates hadn't started the piece yet. Maybe he tossed the pages. What I can know about Jacob Volk is now finite.

The White piece ends with this paragraph:

Lately Jake had been taking life easy. Everybody liked him. He had lots of money. Noons he'd turn up at his Park Avenue office, and eat a caviar sandwich. sitting there in his shirtsleeves. Nights there were fights in the Garden to go to. With all his prosperity he remained a true East Sider in his talk and his way of thinking. He had, however, trod the crumbling ruins of too many haughty dwellings ever to feel

self-conscious or out of place, no matter where he was.
Jake knew that everything that goes up comes down.

At different times in my life I would read the White piece and
see Jake different ways: Jake, the roué; Jake, the wise man; Jake,
the show-off; Jake, the pro. I'd see E. B. White different ways
too. The printed word is labile. It changes as you change. At one
point after reading the piece, I became obsessed with the taste
Jake loved—caviar. Specifically, the caviar sandwich. Was it a
closed sandwich? Was it on soda crackers? Did he dump a tin on
a bialy? Even in a restaurant family caviar is the treat of treats, a
luxury rationed out on crustless toast points. I love its briny taste
and the firecracker sensation as hundreds of slippery eggs from
primeval sturgeon explode in my mouth. I love pressing my
tongue against the roof of my mouth and feeling them pop. It's
like eating the Fourth of July.

Did Jake think about the buildings he tore down,
where the families went? Was he troubled by
this, a professional displacer of people who supported forty-eight
fraternal and philanthropic societies? Did he feel different about
taking down a tenement than taking down a beautiful mansion?
Does a man who flogs his son and pulls his wife's hair worry
about people? I don't know. But I liked that I had an ancestor
who returned to Vilna and built an orphanage. And I liked the
part he played in New York's history, that he literally cleared the
way for the city I live in. You can't build a new city before you
take the old one down. Deconstructionists are not memorialized.
What they do vanishes. They make emptiness. Then something
fills it. So there's nothing you can point to and say, "Look what
Jacob Volk did." But if he could create the space to build a great
city, perhaps I could do something valuable too. No matter what
time period you live in, the opportunity to make your mark, to
do something that matters is there. Making your mark does not
mean making money. It means putting your X on your time.
Inventors do it. Teachers. Lawmakers. Producers. Artists. Sol-

diers. Axe murderers. Everybody's got a shot, even a miller's son from Vilna.

When someone in your family dies before you're born, you know them anecdotally. But if you're lucky, there's another way. If you're lucky, there's written material. And if you're really lucky, some of that material contains quotes. With quotes you get to hear the person's voice, hear him in his own words. There are two quotes that tell me who Jake was better than any story. *Distinguished Jews of America* says he was known as "the Chesterfield of the East Side, for though he could ride a horse, row a boat, play the national game, umpire a boxing bout or act as floor manager of the endless social dances of the district, he was always dressed as the occasion required. Believing that there is a time for work and a time for play, Mr. Volk is sure that 'variation makes you fitted for the sterner battle of life.' "

Jake preferred wrecking skyscrapers to homes. Homes were built to last. When he tore down the W. K. Vanderbilt château on Fifty-second Street, he took a loss. The other words I have out of Jake's mouth came when he was building his house, which still stands, at 2264 Eighty-second Street in Bensonhurst. A friend asked him why he wasn't salvaging the magnificent Vanderbilt interiors to use in his own home. "Listen," said Jake, "am I a piker? You won't see secondhand stuff in my house."

Polly Ann Lieban Morgen, "Best Legs in Atlantic City, 1916"

Everybody did one thing better than anybody else. Aunt Gertie sang the works of Victor Herbert. Aunt Ruthie mamboed. Granny Ethel braked with such finesse it was impossible to tell the moment the car went from moving to a stop. My grandfather was a master bridge-player. My grandmother tied a bow. If you needed a bow tied, if you had anything that would look better with a bow—a hat, a dress, a blouse, a headband, or a handbag—Polly could make and tie the perfect bow for it. Bows of thick satin, quivering organdy, sturdy faille, streaming silk John Singer Sargent bows, striped bows, moiré, breathy tulle, Madame Georgette de la Plante bows. The right bow on the right place could make an outfit. For my sixth-grade graduation Mom picked up a plain white cotton shift. The dress was straight-cut, no frills—a shroud. "Turn around, darling," my grandmother said. She spread her hands around my waist. "Ah. That's it!" She made a wide pale blue satin sash with a notched bow that trailed beyond the hem. The satin looked like water spilling down my waist. The morning of the big event I walked over to her apartment so she could tie it.

It was said of Polly Morgen, "She could do anything with a needle." She could make dresses, and when my mother was little, she stitched up coats with beaver collars, coats with lamb cuffs, coats with seal collars and cuffs. She'd buy a plain cashmere cardigan, then customize it, lining it with lace or chiffon or lace *and* chiffon. Then she'd sew butterfly appliqués or pearls all over it. She sewed so fast her hand was a blur.

"Thread this needle for me, will you, *Zeeseh Kepaleh*?"

I'd thread the needle, proud to help.

"*Vey is meer! Utz a mayor!* In your life! Did you ever see such eyes? *Umbashrign! Gutenyu!* Did you see that, Gert? How my *Bubbaleben* got it *on the first try*?"

My grandmother failed to interest me in mahjong, but she did teach me how to chain stitch, hem, and embroider. On some level I consider myself a failure because I have not been able to teach my children how to sew, not even a button. "Ma!" They bring the shirt to me. "Ma! I have to wear this now!"

"Get the sewing box."

They go to my closet. They take down the box. They sit next to me on the bed and thread the needle, getting it on the first try.

"You've got to learn how to do this yourself," I say, unscrewing the Hellmann's button jar. "Okay, now, make the knot."

They make the knot. They stare at the knot. Then they wail, "I can't do it! Can't you do it for me just this once, Ma? How can you see what's *under*?" "I'm late, Ma." Or just, "Ouch!"

Sewing on a button, like avoiding eye contact on the subway, is a basic life skill. Along with How to Windex a Mirror and How to Make English Muffin Pizza, sewing on a button was taught in the seventh grade by Miss Almeida in home ec. But home ec isn't on New York school curricula anymore. Home ec has gone the way of health class, where we learned you *could* get it from a doorknob.

So my kids can't sew. I've told Polly and Peter if they ever got stranded on a desert island, I might not be there to sew a button on for them. "But Ma," they say, "if we're stranded on a desert island, wouldn't we be more worried about food?" Or "Ma, why would I care about a button? I'd go naked."

So this is what it's come to. I know. I can't teach my children anything they're not absolutely sure they'll need. Their clothes are disposable anyway. It's like when my parents moved to Boca Raton. Something was different. Mom couldn't put her finger on it. Then she needed new lifts on her sandals. That was it. There weren't any shoe repair stores. She asked her tennis partner, "Where do you go in Boca to get your shoes repaired?"

"We don't repair shoes in Boca," the woman replied. "We get new shoes."

I tell my son my mother used to darn socks. "What does 'darn' mean?" Peter says.

I bring a darning egg to my zeitgeist class at Playwrights Horizon Theater School and ask my students what it is. "Maracas?" they say. "A shoe stretcher? Something to mash garlic with?"

We went to Viola Wolff's for social dancing, Helen Rigby's for rhythm and tap, and Madame Svoboda for ballet. Our piano teachers were Cosmé McMoon and Blanche Solomon. Art lessons were on the top floor of the Museum of Modern Art, where your work was exhibited, and parents could say, "My daughter has something in the Museum of Modern Art." We were dilettantes, a little good at a lot of things. I think my mother was raising us to marry kings. When I got too old for the Museum of Modern Art, on Wednesdays my grandmother would take painting lessons with me at the Albert Pels School of Art on West Seventy-first Street. Albert Pels, in his billowing blue smock, was usually working by the window on an epic canvas, copying *Liberty Leading the People* or *The Rape of the Daughters of Leucippus*. His wife, Gloria, drifted from easel to easel offering encouragement and Pepsi in tiny dental-office cups. No matter what Gloria set up on the still-life table, my grandmother painted pink flowers in a blue-and-white vase. At home, with her little wooden box of oils, she painted pink flowers *on* the vase. After art school we'd bus to her apartment and play canasta, and she'd let me win.

"You threw the game!" I'd protest.

"No, light of my life. Would your Nana throw a game?"

"You did! You have two queens! You could have picked the pack!"

"No, *Bubbaleh*. With God as my witness, you won fair and square."

If my sister was there, we'd explore the dramatic potential of the fourth-floor incinerator. We'd throw rice and sog balls (gobs of wet toilet paper) out the living-room window until the doorman sleuthed it out and rang the bell. (Every New York generation throws different things out the window. My mother spit cherry pits. On the East Side they dumped pulp.) If my grandmother was cooking Chicken Fricassee with Meatballs, she would pinch off raw hamburger and feed it to us while we watched her work. I was crazy about the word "fricassee." I was sure it had something to do with what a chicken did or what my grandmother did to the chicken. It wasn't like any other word I knew. The closest I could come was Zuider Zee. Recipes I've tried suggest browning floured and seasoned chicken parts before you stew them. Floured chicken makes a fricassee sound in the pan when you brown it in butter. It splutters. Fricassee! Fricassee! The sauce was emplastic. In her silver well and tree it pooled gray-brown, not the color or texture of any other food we ate. But the meat was so tender it frayed, and the sauce so complex, there were no dull bites. Chicken today, once you get past the skin, tastes like packing pellets. Nana's sauce worked its way to the bone.

Going to my grandmother's house also meant getting checked for a clean hankie because a lady should always carry a clean hankie. She tucked hers up the wrist of her sleeve. Aunt Lil stuffed hers down her cleavage. My mother kept one in her handbag, where it magnetized Pall Mall shreds. Though Dad still gets cotton ones by the dozen from his handkerchief man on the Lower East Side, ladies' hankies have gone the way of "I beg your pardon." Was it germ phobia? The romance of disposables? The time it takes to iron a gossamer roll-hemmed square? Gone with hankies is hankie behavior: daubing and weeping, fanning and wringing. The delicate patting of nostrils. Flailing *au revoir* from the passenger deck of the *Liberté*. The miracle of your mother never failing to find a clean corner she could rub into a point for stabbing soot out of your eye. Covering the hole while you shook a bottle of cool cologne.

My grandmother had a friend she called the handkerchief thief. Amazing since Polly rarely let go of hers. She could extract a hankie from her right sleeve *with her right hand*. She could play canasta with it mashed in the palm she held her cards in. She needed it to laugh. She needed it to cry. It was her resuscitator, her visual italics, her flourish. It was Polly's prop, something to say "Toodle-ooo!" with, what they call "business" on the stage. But in life it bought her time. You could concretize your thoughts while monitoring your hankie. You could pull yourself together.

Except for Desdemona at the Met, I haven't seen a woman use a handkerchief in years. Hankies were the raised pinkie of accessories. Hankie mannerisms would look goofy with ever-ready, proletarian, labor-free Kleenex.

M y grandmother wasn't traditionally religious. She was, however, Orthodox superstitious, glatt superstitious, superstitious beyond black cats and open umbrellas and holding your breath when you passed a cemetery.

"If you come back into the apartment because you forgot something, sit on the bed and count to ten."

"Always lay the opening of a pillowcase *away* from the door."

"If you're waiting for a bus and two go by filled, you can't get on the third even if it's empty, or something bad will happen."

"Never pick up a dropped coin unless it's faceup. Except for quarters."

"Never hand a ring to a friend, or you'll break the friendship."

"If a bird flies into your house, within two days someone you know will die."

"If you're holding hands in the street and a lamppost is about to separate you, say, 'Bread and butter.' "

"Never put a needle on a bed."

"Stepping over someone's legs will stunt his growth."

"Spit through your fingers three times to ward off the evil eye."

"Tie a red ribbon on a baby's crib to ward off the evil eye."

"When giving a compliment, say, '*Kine horah*,' to ward off the evil eye."

My grandfather refused to open a store in a building with a thirteenth floor. The elevator had to read 11, 12, 14, 15. If a reservation came in for a party of thirteen, he'd write "12 + 1" or "14 − 1" in the book. His son knocked wood three times before picking up the phone.

Superstition is contagious. It's the original quid pro quo: You don't do this, and that won't happen. You *do* do that, and this will happen. It isn't like faith. With faith, you have to trust God. With superstition, it's cause and effect. I didn't walk under a ladder! I'm still alive! It worked!

My grandmother had her own ideas about health too. She pushed her children in their strollers at six in the morning "before the air got used." If you drank too much water, you had diabetes. She would take me to lunch and say, "Order anything you want, darling." When I asked for a hamburger, she'd say, "The meat could be spoiled." So I'd ask for chopped egg, and she'd say, "How do we know the eggs are fresh?" So I'd try for tuna, and she'd say, "What if the mayonnaise is rancid?" and I'd wind up with a grilled cheese.

N ana was the person you came to when you needed help. She was a problem-solver. She found jobs for people. She lent money with no expectations. Every Thanksgiving, Morgen's Sandwich Shop at 1214 Broadway and Morgen's Grill at 176 Fifth Avenue would officially close, but Nana would patrol Ninth and Tenth Avenues distributing two hundred Morgen's meal tickets to the "needy and destitute of the community," according to the *Evening World*. Morgen's would be open for anyone she could find who needed a turkey dinner. Once, she saw a man leaving the store with no coat. "Here," she said, handing him my grandfather's new vicuna. "This will keep you warm." My mother's birthday parties were celebrated at the Hebrew Orphan Asylum of the City of New York on Amsterdam Avenue and 137th Street. She'd share her cake with the "inmates," as the *World Telegram & Sun* referred to them. Whatever birthday my mother had, my grandmother doubled the number in inmates. When Mom turned nine, there were eighteen. The newspapers liked to cover the event and would name the orphans in print: Arthur Engel, Herbert Zuckerman, Morris Ennes, John Goldberg, Estelle Cohen, Morris Levy, Gertrude Marlin, Ruth Stork, Nathan Katz, Maggie Finkle. Everybody got presents. They'd tell stories and play games.

L ong after she didn't have to save money, my grandmother kept saving it. All leftover vegetables went into succotash. She rinsed out tinfoil and hung it up to dry. Grapefruit seeds rarely made it to the garbage. She sprouted them on wet cotton balls, then planted them in pots filled with free dirt from Central Park. She never gave up the dream of a fruit-bearing grapefruit tree on a New York windowsill.

L ike Ethel Volk, Nana was seventeen when she married my grandfather. They met on a blind date arranged by her older sister, Gertie. At the end of the evening Herman turned to Polly and said, "I recently met a woman, and I'm in love with her. I'm going to propose, and if she says no, I'm leaving town."

"Kiss me, darling," Nana said. "I know you mean me."

She'd already had two proposals. One from a dentist named Irving. She accepted, then changed her mind. When he yelled up from the street for her to come down, she flung her engagement ring out the window.

Maurice she never said yes to. He took her for a ride in Central Park at night, then stopped the car in a dark place.

"I ran out of gas," he said, sliding his arm around her.

"Take me home!" Nana pulled away. "My fortune is my reputation, and my reputation is my fortune!"

I loved this sentence. It was perfect. Not only could you learn from it, it was reversible.

Maurice proposed, but Polly turned him down too. Then she went to city hall with my grandfather and got a marriage license. His name was Herman Morgenbesser (Morning Kisser), but after studying the way it looked, she said, "Herman, your name is too long for America." She drew a line through the "besser." From then on, they were Polly and Herman Morgen.

They married on September 10 in Auverne, Queens, where Polly's parents had rented a summerhouse. Her braids were still wet from a morning dip in the Atlantic. Like most women of her day, she didn't swim. She waded out holding a knotted rope tied to a pier. As Herman was driving Polly to the ceremony, Maurice jumped on the running board. He hung there, rapping on the window, begging my grandmother not to go through with it. Herman swerved him off. In the backseat, his future in-laws, Jenny and Louis Lieban, sat holding hands. They needed a vacation so they came along on the honeymoon. The four of them passed a pleasant week at the Half Moon Hotel on Coney Island.

I wear the bracelet Great-grandma Jenny had made before she married Louis. Nine dimes, linked, each engraved with the initials of a friend. Elaborate hand-carved initials on the "tails" side of a Liberty dime. They don't immediately read "dimes." Polly had the bracelet dipped in gold. She loved all things gold: doré lamps, bangles by the armload, glittery glasses, ormolu.

Herman Morgen was so grateful to have won my grandmother's heart, he promised God he would give something up. It had to be something he loved, something he'd miss every waking day. It had to be a genuine sacrifice. And so it came to pass that my grandfather gave up pork, his favorite food in the world. No more spareribs, no more roast loin, no more bratwurst, *choucroute garnie*, grilled pork chops, hocks in brown sauce, trotters, pigs' knuckles, or Italian pork sausage. No more fricadeller or knockwurst in beer or *tourtière* (pork pie). No more nonkosher salami! No more holiday ham! No more bacon! That

was it. In exchange for the gift of my grandmother, he would sati-
ate the jealous gods by giving up something of equal worth. He
officially gave up pork and all pork by-products. So the fact that
he continued to eat liverwurst baffled me. Did he, the restaurant
man, not know that liverwurst was made from the liver of a pig?
Was it possible that he blanked that out, had a little blind spot? Or
was it that he gave up pork *with one exception*, that it was enough
to give up the *majority* of pork. No one asked him. No one talked
about it. Once, watching him bite into slabs of liverwurst squeezing
through the edges of ebony pumpernickel slathered with Thousand Island dressing from Morgen's that was so rich we called it
Million Island dressing, I said, "Poppy, what's liverwurst made of?"

"Liver, darling," he said.

I watched his face. He was loving that sandwich. I thought
about saying, "Liver of what?"

To prevent slipping, the terra-cotta tiles on the
kitchen floor at Morgen's were covered with wood
pallets. Somehow my grandmother fell on some fat. Doctors
nailed her hip back together. She would break it once more, this
time tumbling down the stairs at our house. I was there. I saw her
land. Splayed on the carpet, she said, "Don't worry, darling. I
won't sue." She laughed. From then on, she limped. She described
herself as "lame." She learned to live with the compromise of pain.
It was a mean irony that the woman who was voted "Best Legs in
Atlantic City" in 1916 should have one turn against her. Although
I was five or six the first time she broke her hip, I couldn't remember her walking without hiking the bad hip up and swinging the
leg forward. Then we had the family Kodachromes transferred to
tape, and there she was, skipping down a flagstone path, laughing,
her black curls bouncing, raising her skirt, showing the kind of leg
that used to be called well turned, a leg carved on a lathe.

"*Bubbaleben*, rub my leg!" she'd call from her gray bedroom.
I'd run in and dive my hand up to the elbow in a gallon jar of
Pond's cold cream. She'd be stretched out in her bathrobe, her
housekeeper, Lilly, watching from the door.

"Harder! Higher!" Nana would say. Or "Oh, my *laben*-on-the-*kepaleh*, my *zeeseh kinder*, that's good!"

I'd rub from the ankle to the hip. She'd moan. The rubbing would last until the last whiteness of the Pond's sank into her shiny shin. Then she would flap the robe closed.

"Did you ever do the leg?" I ask my sister.

"I loved doing the leg," my sister tells me.

I must have loved doing the leg too, or I would have found a way out of it.

Her pain got so bad she took pills that sounded like miracle fibers, Darvon and Percodan. When it became unbearable, she began the New York medical hejira. She took her hip X rays to all the orthopedic stars in the city. The "top men" all said the same thing: It was hopeless. The pin had deteriorated and the bone too. There was nothing they could do. If they tried to take the pin out, the bone would shatter and she'd never walk again.

If you look long and hard enough in New York, you can always find someone to say yes. Dr. Bosworth at St. Luke's was willing to give it a shot. During the procedure her hipbone crumbled into gravel. She spent her last six years in bed with round-the-clocks. Lilly would greet us at the door, and I'd smell the smell. It wasn't the rich kitchen smell anymore. It was the stale smell of medicine and cold cream and dust in the drapes mixed with food ground into the wall-to-wall by nurses who knew they weren't coming back.

"Put an ice cube in my tea!" Nana would call to them.

"Put more hot water in my tea!"

"Who made the tea?"

"Fluff my pillows."

"Bring a cookie for the baby!"

"Not that kind of cookie!"

"Not that kind of cookie!"

"Where's the Arrowroot? Who ate the Arrowroot?"

I would sit by her bed showing off my son, asking what I could do. I couldn't do anything.

"AN ARROWROOT FOR THE BABY! SOMEBODY! *PLEASE!*"

Violet or Sabina or Lucille would scurry into the kitchen and come back with the wrong cookie.

"Nana," I told her, pressing her hand against my belly, "if it's a girl, I'm going to name her after you. I love the name Polly."

"Is that right, darling? Tell Violet I need more tea."

My Polly was born four months after Polly died of kidney failure from a rampant staph infection. Mom buried her in her favorite robe, white eyelet with a blue satin bow at the neck. Jewish law dictates that a body be interred without delay. When possible, Jewish people bury their dead within twenty-four hours. My grandmother's will stipulated that we wait three days. She was born in 1899, the time of Queen Victoria. There was no medically reliable way, except putrefaction, to be sure a person was definitely dead. So many people had been buried alive, so many coffins had been opened with scratch marks inside the lids that English coffins came with an aboveground bell, the pull placed in the hand of the deceased, just in case.

On February 8, 1964, the Beatles came to town for their first appearance on *The Ed Sullivan Show*. They were going to stay at The Plaza. My younger cousins Joanie and Marcy convinced Nana to take them to Fifty-ninth Street in hopes of catching a glimpse. Mounted police high-stepped through the screaming crowd. Barricades were everywhere. Nana and the girls couldn't get closer than The Sherry-Netherland. A rumor spread that the Beatles were going to wave from a window. It was freezing cold. My grandmother stood for almost an hour. Finally she couldn't take it anymore.

"Look!" Nana shouted.

"Where?" Joanie and Marcy yelled.

"Look! They waved!" Nana said. "You saw them!"

"We did?"

"Yes, girls! You saw them! Okay, who wants hot chocolate at Rumpelmayer's?"

When we got lost in a bog last summer, my sister said,
"If I die first, you can eat me."

HERSHEYETTES

My mother calls to tell me my sister weighs 150 pounds: "I don't think her husband could like it very much," my mother says. "Do you?"

My sister calls to tell me she's starting Jenny Craig: "I met with my diet counselor and told her she could have every piece of jewelry I had on if she could get me thin enough to wear her jeans."

The next morning my sister calls to tell me the diet's not working: "You have to buy all the food from Jenny Craig, and it's horrible."

"My friend Brenda is on the English Red and Green Diet," I tell her. "You eat five fruits and five veggies every day. But on green days you add things that grow. And on red days you add things that walk."

"I don't need a diet," my sister says. "I know every diet. Here's the trick, okay? Here's all you have to know: Eat less."

Since my sister and I like to invent things—Cuzzles, the Cookie Puzzle for Kids; the *10 Meals in 10 Minutes for 10 Dollars*

Cookbook revised to the *20 Meals in 20 Minutes for 20 Dollars Cookbook;* the book about sisters somebody else did; the movie about sisters we didn't know enough about movies to make; reading glasses that beep when you press a locator button so you can find them; the Hoseable Apartment, where floors gently slope toward a drain and everything is waterproof, even the books; Airplane Dating so when you book your seat, you get to say what kind of person you'd like to sit next to—since we like to hatch schemes, I say, "Why don't we do a book of all the diets we've been on? Fifty-two diets, a new one every week."

We start naming diets: The Nine-Egg-a-Day, the Grapefruit, the Beverly Hills, the Atkins, the Modified Atkins, the Ornish, the Pineapple, the Scarsdale, the Sauerkraut, the Red Soup, the Mayo Clinic, the Duke Rice Diet, the Vanderbilt Rotation Diet, the Hilton Head Metabolism Diet, the Substitution Diet, Weight Watchers, Weight Watchers Quick Start, the Watermelon, the Loma Linda, Fit for Life, Sugar Busters!, Dr. Hevert's Famous Diet (modified Atkins), the Chew Everything 30 Times Diet, the Blood-type Diet, the Bloomingdale's Eat Healthy Diet, Dr. Berger's Immune Power Diet, Dr. McDougall's 12-Day Diet Meal Plan, the Carbohydrate Addicts Diet, the Hollywood 48-Hour Miracle Diet (ten pounds in a weekend), the Cyberdiet, the Stillman, Optifast, Dexfenfluramine HCI, the Nutri/System Diet Plan, the Zone Diet, Medifast, Metrecal, Slim-Fast, Ultra Slim-Fast, Richard Simmons Deal-A-Meal, the 8-Glasses-of-Water-a-Day, the Pritikin Diet, HMV, Horse Hoof Protein, the Liquid Protein. I especially like the one where you eat nothing but fruit till noon and then all the protein you want. Or all the protein you want till noon, and nothing but fruit the rest of the day. One diet my sister was on allowed her to eat unlimited bacon. Microwaves had just come out. She kept those rashers going in on paper towels. DING! Four rashers came out, four rashers went in. For dinner she ate steak with a sooty black crust. The weight fell off. Her breath smelled like nail polish remover. "That was the Acetone Breath Diet," my sister says. "Do you think I have A.D.D.?"

"Attention Deficit Disorder?"

"Attention *Diet* Disorder," she says.

When you watch your weight, you literally watch it. We are masters of the scale. Bend one knee, you weigh less. Lean sideways, that's worth a pound. If you weigh yourself before breakfast after going to the bathroom and walking twice around the reservoir, that's the least you'll weigh all day. You weigh less after a shower than you do before, provided your hair is dry. If you hold your breath and suck in your gut, the needle on the scale heads west. You can weigh less from blowing your nose, brushing your teeth, cutting your cuticles, and thinking light thoughts. You can lose (or gain) weight stepping off the scale, then getting right back on.

People like my sister and me know our weight at any given time. The sixth grade, before the musical at camp, during the SATs, first day of college, first date with husband-to-be, wedding weight, post-honeymoon weight, pre- and post-baby weights, weight at grandmother's funeral. Give us a year, we'll give it back to you in pounds. Give us a *day*.

"We've had thirty years of fat and thin," my sister says.

"I've got a distorted body image," I tell her. "I think I look good."

Weight was never not an issue. It was there, every morning, like the *New York Times*. At Weight Watchers they tell you, "Nothing tastes as good as thin feels." But my sister has decided she prefers eating to looking skinny, that eating gives her more pleasure, even if she wears only bespoke black. Once, when we rented a movie, she bought a bag of Hershey's Hugs. I told her not to buy anything Hershey, because when I'd done the advertising for the company, I'd invented the name Hershey's Hugs for a candy to be sold alongside Hershey's Kisses—Hugs and Kisses—and I never got credit for it. I did get credit for inventing the name "Whatchamacallit" for a new candy bar. "Hershey's Whatchamacallit. You can ask for it by name," the logo line went. It was my major contribution in eighteen years of advertising. But Hershey stole the Hugs name, so I've been boycotting them for twelve years. "If you buy Hugs," I told my sister, "it's the same as crossing a picket line. If you buy Hugs, you're a scab."

She bought the Hugs. In the car she unwrapped eight and palmed them into her mouth.

"Why are you doing that?" I asked her.

"I love the sensation of the chocolate filling my mouth, the area around my teeth, of it melting on my tongue, and sliding hot and liquidy down my throat. I love the taste. I love the feel."

What could I say? By the time she pulled into her driveway, the bag was empty.

In 1996, while cleaning out a dresser drawer, I came across a small locked metal box. The box had moved to four apartments with me. I couldn't remember the last time I'd seen it. I shook it in my hand. Something was inside. It sounded like paper. A hundred-dollar bill? A secret? A last will and testament? On top of my dresser there's a small tray filled with mystery keys. I tried the little ones. None of them worked. I got a screwdriver. That didn't work either. Finally I pried the box open with the claw of a hammer. Inside, there was a yellowed three-by-five card. Written on it were the words "All-time High: 143."

By the fourth grade my sister was taller than all her teachers. She's still tall. Recently she had her skeleton weighed. A doctor glued electrodes over key bones and ran a charge through them. "It felt prickly," she says. "Like when your foot falls asleep, then starts to wake up." A strip of paper chattered out of the machine. My sister's skeleton weighed 117 pounds. The doctor was stunned. "For a person your height," he said, "your skeleton should weigh eighty-eight. This is the largest female skeleton I've ever seen." So now at least we have proof: My sister is big-boned.

In high school we dieted in earnest. We wore full skirts with crinolines made rigid by soaking them in a bathtub full of sugar water. Then we'd tuck in a sweater or blouse and buckle on a four-inch cinch belt. Because the skirts ballooned out, our waists looked tiny. My sister could get hers down to twenty-two inches. I could get mine under twenty. Still we thought we were fat.

There was an obstetrician/gynecologist in town who stopped doing ob/gyn to become a diet specialist full-time. Dad went to him and started losing weight. We convinced Mom to take us. The doctor prescribed a small pink pill. A lot of girls in our high school were taking the small pink pill. It made you not interested in food. You just didn't think about it. When you went for fries after school, they lacked appeal. When you went for pizza after the movies, you couldn't finish a slice. The weight fell off. Desserts lost their glow. Our waists got smaller. People stopped us to tell us how thin we were. The first week, I lost 8½ pounds, my sister, 7. The doctor praised us. He prescribed more pink pills. Mother seemed pleased. Even so, she kept our chocolate shelves loaded.

The pink pills had no impact on our need for chocolate. There was a small cabinet in the kitchen. The upper shelf was for my sister's Tootsie Rolls, the bottom shelf was for my Hersheyettes. Hersheyettes were the Hershey Company's answer to M&M's. They were drops of chocolate covered with a pastel sugar shell stamped H. Three things set Hersheyettes apart: one, the Hershey association. Two, the sugar shells were Easter colors—pink, lavender, baby blue. And three, the shape was unusual—two small cones stuck together at their wide part. Looking head-on at a Hersheyette, it was shaped like a diamond. I preferred the chocolate in M&M's. But there was more to Hersheyettes. You could spin them on your tongue like a top.

Hersheyettes seemed to take off. During my senior year in high school, they replaced M&M's in the vending machines at

Jones Beach. I thought I'd always have them. On Mom's weekly visits to the supermarket, she'd pick me up a one-pound bag. She wanted us to lose weight, she was happy we were successes at the diet doctor's, but she understood the need for chocolate too. Besides, even with the candy, as long as you took a little pink pill every day, you'd keep losing weight. My candy shelf was well stocked. Then I left for college, and when I came home for Thanksgiving, Hersheyettes had vanished.

In college I made an accidental discovery. I forgot to take a pink pill one morning. When I remembered, it was late afternoon. That night, I couldn't sleep. If you took a pink pill late in the day, it kept you up. You could pull an all-nighter. Something in the diet doctor's pink pills made it possible to study all night before a final. You didn't feel sleepy at all. If anything, you felt energized and smarter.

The disappearance of Hersheyettes is a mystery. It may have been a shelf-space problem. Shelf space in the supermarket is an ongoing, filthily fought, kill-or-get-killed battle. Often a new product can launch itself by out-couponing preexisting products. Consumers will keep buying the new product despite brand loyalty to the old product because the new one is so much cheaper with a coupon. The company giving the discount coupon is willing to take a loss because it's hard to change established buying patterns, especially for "parity" products like glass cleaners or club soda or a tiny sugarcoated milk chocolate candy. The Mars Company, which puts out M&M's, may have fought back with its own coupon war. No Hersheyettes ad campaign comes to mind like the M&M spot with the little naked M&M and its friend the peanut M&M diving into a swimming pool of chocolate. "First we're drenched in creamy milk chocolate," the plain M&M, the brainy one, says. They grab the pool ladder and swing their little chocolate bodies back and forth until all the extra chocolate flies off and they zip up their sugar shells. "Melts in your mouth, not in your hand."

In the end, what may have killed Hersheyettes was unmemorable advertising. Or poor distribution. Or maybe not enough people liked them. You'd think anyone who liked a Hershey bar would have liked Hersheyettes. The Hershey name has chocolate equity. Hershey *means* chocolate. M&M's don't have any chocolate connection or brand-name recognition beyond M&M's. So Hersheyettes should have been a natural, a "line extension," like Wrigley's spearmint gum coming out with a breath mint. Or Nike bridging the Dr. Scholl's or Spenco market. The Hershey name alone was permission to believe a Hersheyette would be a morsel of America's favorite candy bar. And that may have been the problem. When I did the advertising for Hershey, I was told that not all Hershey milk chocolate is the same. Premium milk chocolate goes into the gold-wrapped candy, a lesser grade is used for the familiar brown- and silver-wrapped bars. When other flavors are added, say wafers with KitKat or puffed rice and penuche with Whatchamacallit, the quality of the chocolate plummets. Hershey uses cheaper chocolate with a lower cocoa fat content in these bars because consumers can't tell the chocolate isn't first-rate when it's mixed with so much other stuff. The worst chocolate goes into Mr. Goodbar, Chicago's number-one candy bar. The peanuts taste so strong, people don't notice the chocolate's not up to speed. A Hersheyette tasted different from a Hershey bar.

Hersheyettes vanished. The little pink pills disappeared too. Preludins turned out to be amphetamines that caused birth defects. The diet doctor lost his New York State license in a sting. He sold one thousand Preludins to a federal agent. He moved to California, got a license there, and went back to the practice of obstetrics and gynecology. I stopped taking Preludins eight years before I had children. My kids seem pretty normal despite the airbrushed perfectionism of their supermodel norm, despite growing up without ever seeing an unwanted hair, the heartbreak of psoriasis, a cellulite dimple, or a backside you could serve tea off of.

Herman Morgen, the first man to carve meat in a window

CHOPPED LIVER

Grapefruit was the medicine of food.

"Please, darling, please," my grandfather begged. "Just one bite. For *me*?" I didn't get it. Why would anybody voluntarily eat pulp? Orange juice was strained to get the pulp *out*. The sensation of sour bursting beads in the mouth was more repulsive than sand in a sandwich at the beach.

"Darling, one bite. That's all I ask. If you don't like it, you don't have to finish it."

Why was grapefruit worth so much discussion? Why all this pleading over a fruit? Then I figured it out: Our blood was stored in tiny thin-skinned pointy sacs too. When you scraped your knee, it eventually stopped bleeding because the damaged sacs had a limit. Once the wound reached intact sacs, the bleeding stopped. Inside, humans were like grapefruits, and you needed grapefruit to keep you that way.

Herman Morgen started every Thursday night dinner at his table with half a grapefruit. There were always six courses: grapefruit, chopped liver, soup or tomato juice, salad, an entrée with a starch and at least two vegetables, one of which was string beans *almondine au beurre noisette,* and three or four desserts, two of which were my grandmother's apple pie and lemon meringue pie and in season, strawberry shortcake.

Sometimes my grandfather ate his grapefruit broiled with caramelized sugar on top. Sometimes he ate it cold with a maraschino cherry. First he'd dig out the precut segments with a serrated grapefruit spoon. Then he'd take the grapefruit in his left hand and squeeze whatever droplets were left into his grapefruit spoon. When that was done, he'd excavate the rind. The only other person I knew who ate a grapefruit as thoroughly was my upstairs friend Alice Shapera's older brother, Bob. On Friday nights in apartment 13F Bob went one step further. After decimating the grapefruit, he wore the hollowed rind on his head like a yarmulke. Eventually Bob changed his last name to Evans, became a producer in Hollywood, and married Ali McGraw.

Hello, Poppy?"
       "Yes, darling."
"If I come down to the store around two thirty, could you have lunch with me?"
SLAM.
My grandfather didn't say good-bye when he hung up the phone. *SLAM* meant yes, it was fine for me to stop by for lunch. And yes, he'd be able to sit down with me after the last (which on a good day meant third) turnover. Who needs good-bye? Why waste time? If you slam down the phone, the conversation is over.

When he wasn't in the store, my grandfather took things slower. Sniffing his cigar. Rolling it between his fingers. Clipping, licking, lighting it. Pondering its ash. Eating. Herman Morgen was a trencherman, a volume eater. He leaned into his plate. He liked to eat, but he wasn't fat. He was five feet nine but he looked taller. His eyes were pewter. His upper lids had a fold that made him look as if he could see through you, see things you didn't know about yourself. He had heavy brows, full lips, and smooth rosy cheeks. Herman Morgen was neat. He smelled good. He radiated a manly cleanliness and walked with his chest out. Overall he gave the impression of being robust, a man with a limitless peak and low tolerance for fools. He refused Novocain at the dentist's. He kept a pebble in his shoe to remind himself to stand straight and suggested I do the same. He wore immaculately tailored suits. When he came home in a new gray silk from Saks, my grandmother, whose syntax was based on the hyperbolic compliment, said, "Herman! You look so handsome! You should have bought *three* of those!"

He went back to Saks and ordered two more.

He loved work. He loved to walk fast, then recuperate on a bench and turn his face to the sun. Above all, he loved to play bridge.

"Like shooting fish in a barrel," he'd whisper to me, fanning out a hand.

It's stunning to me now that I loved him unequivocally. He could have a flinty heart. He failed to appreciate my father and was less than loving. With the exception of my mother and grandmother, people seemed afraid of him. Once, I was sitting on the Madison Avenue bus, and he boarded at Fifty-second Street. He didn't see me right away. I never imagined he used public transportation. In the moment before I knew it was my grandfather, I thought, There's a powerful man.

He was proud of his restaurants and part of that pride depended on the concept of the satisfied customer. "A fellow came in. Ordered Prime Rib. Ate it all except for one bite. Then he sent the bite back. 'Too well done,' he said."

"Poppy! What did you do?"

"I asked him if I could get him something else, darling. Told him I was sorry. Took it off the check."

This is not to say the customer was always right. He would look a rude one in the eye and say, "You know that revolving door that brought you in? It'll take you back out. And when you see black crepe hanging in the window, you'll know I miss you."

When my grandfather first started working in restaurants, his boss told him something that became a Herman Morgen business tenet. "Sheeny," the man said, "here's some advice: When you give people something for free, make it good or don't bother." In the spirit of making what's free good, the bar at cocktail hour offered free coconut shrimp, miniature potato pancakes, skewered scallops grilled with pineapple, marinated chicken wings, sweet and pungent meatballs. Tables in the dining room were set with silver salvers of celery hearts, pickled peppers, radishes carved into roses, full sours, and mammoth green salty olives on a blizzard of crushed ice, alps of ice, fabulous ice that sent a cool breeze over the table when the waiter swooped it down. The breadbasket teetered with Parker House rolls, caraway salt crescents, raisin bread, sesame sticks, Ry-Krisp, and onion bread baked in the store with the onions blackened first in chicken fat. *Garni* on an entrée meant more than a parsley sprig: scarlet cinnamon-soaked crab apples; a nest of watercress; chiffonades, kumquats, riced egg, diced peppers, a perfect pickled green tomato.

You could make a meal out of what the store gave away and some people did. As a business strategy, this was confusing. Why serve free food if you make your living selling it?

"Darling," my grandfather said, "the big profit in the restaurant business doesn't come from food. It comes from the bar." Years later, when the ad agency I worked for pitched the Ponderosa Steak-House account, I did steak-house research. I learned that the steak at fast-food steak houses was a freebie. They bought low-grade meat by the ton and used time and chemicals to tenderize it in stainless-steel vats. You could give the steak away as long as the customer bought a Coke. The Coke cost Ponderosa less than a penny.

Herman Morgen was twelve when he immigrated to America. His parents had sent him to boarding school, and he was miserable. It was the kind of boarding school where your family supplied the board. Since his parents owned an inn, sending food to their son was no problem. But what they sent was intercepted and little of it reached him.

"They never gave me enough to eat," my grandfather said. "Sweetheart, I was starving."

His older brother, Leopold, was already in America. My grandfather boarded a ship and came alone to New York. Leaning over the railing, watching the Statue of Liberty fade in and out of the mist, he swore he would never speak German or Polish again, that the little town he came from in the Tatra Mountains would no longer be part of his life. He would never go back, never see his parents. Herman Morgen would be an American now. He would bathe every day. He would chew gum. He moved in with Leopold until their father sent a letter: "I can't have two boys in America," it said. "I need one home."

My grandfather didn't want to go back. Back to what? A school that was unbearable and a father fond of the strap? Leopold was the older brother. "You would be more useful," Herman said. Leopold went back.

Herman Morgen's first job was sweeping up in a restaurant. When he mastered that, he got promoted to stuffing coleslaw into pleated paper cups. By the time he was fourteen, he was a prep man. The next year, line cook. At sixteen he moved onto the floor, rising from busboy to waiter in less than a year. That's when he got a brainstorm: Since people eat with their eyes, why not show them something? He was working at a café on Times Square. The window was filled with snake plants. He moved the plants and replaced them with a roasted steamship round (the full thigh, top and bottom of a steer). He tied on an apron and borrowed a *toque blanche*. Then he sharpened his knives and began carving for the crowds on Broadway. People stopped. They stared. They watched piece after piece of perfectly sliced steaming pink meat fall. They stood on their toes to see. My grandfather said they watched that meat the way, sixty years later, people watched Neil Armstrong walk on the moon. He was the first man to carve meat in a window. It brought the customers in.

Herman Morgen was elevated to assistant manager. Then manager. By twenty-four he was making enough money to get married. When he was ready to open his own store, Polly, who all her life used a tea bag twice, handed him a stack of bankbooks held together with a rubber band. She was a genius at saving money. He opened Morgen's Sandwich Shop at 1214 Broadway.

Over the years Herman Morgen owned fourteen stores in New York: Robert's Tavern (where Uncle Bob was a busboy), Robert's Bake Shop, Robert's Seafood, Morgen's, Morgen's East, Morgen's Sandwich Shop, Morgen's Café (managed by my grandmother), Herman's Cafeteria (bought for his sister Broncha to run), Herman's Coffee Shoppe, Herman's Café (managed by his sister's husband), Herman's Tavern (managed by my great-grandfather), Herman's Luncheonette (opened for Aunt Gertie's husband), Herman's Grill, and Hergen's. Anyone who needed a job got a restaurant.

"Everyone in the family took from him," Dad says. "He was there. He was generous."

Only once did he get duped. A restaurant at the Brooklyn Navy Yard was for sale. He went to see what kind of lunch it did. The place was packed. The line was out the door. He bought the restaurant. When he reopened it, no one came. The previous owner had "loaded" the house. He'd filled it with friends to make the restaurant look busy. "Your grandfather worked like a slave to build that place up so he could sell it," my father says. "He lived there. He *slept* there. He did everything."

When my grandfather hit me, he was baby-sitting for ten days while my parents were on a cruise to Curaçao. It was Sunday night. We were going to Ruby Foo's on West Fifty-second Street, the only Chinese restaurant we ate at because of the rumor they used cats in China-town.

I began to get ready.

"Brush your teeth," my grandfather said.

"I never brush my teeth before dinner, Poppy."

"I said, Brush your teeth."

"I only brush my teeth in the morning and before bed."

"I said, Brush them!"

I explained that according to my mother, I only had to brush my teeth twice a day.

"No," my grandfather said. "You have to brush them now, before we go to Ruby Foo's."

"No. I don't. I only have to brush my teeth once before break-fast and once before bed." I told him I'd be happy to comb my hair though. "Want me to comb my hair, Poppy? I'll comb my hair."

He followed me into the bathroom. My sister watched from her bed, where she sat eating a raw onion sandwich to clear her nasal passages. I stood on my toes and reached for the comb on the black glass shelf below the medicine chest.

"See?" I said. "I'm combing my hair."

"Brush your teeth."

"But I don't have to."

"I said, Brush your teeth."

"Want me to wash my hands, Poppy? I'll wash my hands."

That's when he hit me. He hit the side of my face. The hit lifted me. Landing on the tiled bathroom floor, I was aware of coolness places my undershirt wasn't. My arms, my neck, the back of my legs. Then I opened my eyes and saw the underside of our pedestal sink. It was gray like pavement, only rough like my mother's broadtail coat. So this is what the underside of a sink looks like, I thought. I never would have seen the underside of a sink if my grandfather hadn't hit me.

My sister ran to get my grandmother. Something was going to be different. Something would never be the same. Someone could almost bruise you with hard kisses. Someone could smile and say "Jewish fella" when Eddie Fisher came on *The Ed Sullivan Show,* and it would make your day. You'd watch for that smile. If you were sitting behind him, you'd watch to see if the crest of his cheekbone rose. Someone could hug you till you begged for air, then send you flying.

"You weren't hit," my sister says now. "You were walloped."

"I was?"

"He hit you over and over again."

"I don't remember that."

"After that, I knew I'd always have to be good around him. After that, I was scared of him. I thought, You have to do everything a grown-up says. You have to do it, or you get hurt."

When my mother came home, I told her what happened. I wanted to plead my case, to let her know it wasn't my fault I'd gotten hit because she'd told me I only had to brush my teeth twice a day. I was being good, not brushing my teeth a third time. I was following orders.

My grandfather stared at the floor. "You did what?" Mom detonated. "Don't you ever . . . !" "If you so much as ever . . . !" It was the only time I heard someone speak harshly to him. He was unthreatenable, a man free of self-doubt. But he cared what my mother thought about him, so he hung his head. I felt sorry for him and wanted to make it up to him. I would sit on his lap and ride his knee. I would ask about the Yankees. When we walked up and down Riverside Drive at night with nothing to say to each other, when I gave up trying to think of something, anything to interest him, to make him talk to me, when all that was left to do was count the red neon Spry signs blinking on and off across the Hudson in New Jersey, I would squeeze his hand every now and then to remind him I was there and still loved him. I would never complain about the river-blasted wind. And from the night he hit me, from that night on, he would call me by name.

"Patty, darling, could you get me a beer?" and I'd run to his round-shouldered refrigerator and pull out a Miller High Life. "Patty, sweetheart, I could use something cold," and I'd drop my SlapJack cards and pour him a White Rock ginger ale with ice. My sister couldn't race me anymore, because he used my name. He didn't say, "Darling, could you get me a beer?" He said, "Patty."

"Poppy's nicer to you since the hitting," my sister said, punching me on the thigh.

"You could learn a lot from him, you know," I said, grabbing her wrist with my fingernails.

Naturally I swore I'd never hit my kids. I'd make mistakes, just not that one. How could I do anything to them I hated done to me? I would never say, "None of your business." Or "Because I said so." I would never hit. Until I did.

It was almost midnight. First Polly needed water. Then she forgot to feed the fish. Then she forgot to turn the closet light off. Then she thought she saw a roach. Then she needed the closet light on. Then she forgot to pack her book bag. Then she remembered she'd forgotten to tighten her dental appliance. Then she couldn't find her library book. Then she wanted more water. Then I hit her. I didn't know I did it till I'd done it. I hit my child. I lost control. Would she be afraid of me? Would she think of me as the Hand Out of Nowhere? What if she thought she *deserved* being hit?

"I will never forget this moment as long as I live!" she said, pulling the covers up to her chin.

"Oh God, Pussycat. I'm sorry," I said. "I'm so exhausted! It's almost one o'clock! You're wearing me out! I want to live to be an old lady!"

"And I want to live to be ten," she said.

We started to laugh. It seemed less bad.

"I love you more than every pine needle on every pine tree there ever was," I said.

"I love you more than every hair on every head," she said.

"Well, I love you more than every pea in every pod."

I tucked her in, stuck my nose in her hair, then kissed her good night.

"I may have laughed," she whispered in my ear, "but I'm never going to forget you hit me."

"I know that," I said.

M y grandfather did not go to *shul*. He observed being Jewish two ways: On Yom Kippur he fasted all day and broke it by tossing back a jigger of slivovitz at sundown. And every night he prayed. I wouldn't have known this if I hadn't slept over. My grandmother would set up a cot between their twin beds. She made a tight bed with starched white sheets and a dense camel-colored Austrian blanket trimmed in velvet, said to cure arthritis. The bed was so pretty I hated to disturb it. I would tip myself up at the head, then tunnel in without rumpling the covers. "Herman," my grandmother would say, "she's like a worm! Did you ever?"

"Never!" he would say.

Before they turned out the lights, my grandfather would reappear in a sleeveless ribbed undershirt, boxer shorts, a gray homburg, and dark socks held up by garters. He'd pace back and forth at the foot of the beds, head bent, lips moving, an Amen blurted here and there. Then he would peel off his socks, place his hat on the dresser, and turn out the light.

"Colgate-Palmolive?" he would call from his bed.

"Up a quarter, darling."

"Standard Oil of New Jersey?"

"Down an eighth."

"Georgia Pacific?"

"Up three quarters."

"Texaco?"

"Up a half."

So this, I thought, is what married people do.

When my grandfather tripped and broke a rib in the store, he didn't complain. "There's nothing you can do for a broken rib, darling," he explained. But he winced when he laughed, and he groaned when he coughed. Then he began to cough more. Finally, the doctor told us. He had cancer of the pleura, the tissue that surrounds the lungs.

I would visit him in Polyclinic in the West Fifties, the hospital I was born in. He would submit to needle aspirations with no anesthesia, the insertion of various drains and punch biopsies. He couldn't wait to get back to the store. He didn't know he never would.

No one told him he had cancer. It was my mother's decision. He would live longer not knowing he was dying. He would be happier. He would live "not giving up." He would die optimistic.

"What's wrong with me, darling?" he would persist.

"It's an infection," we'd say. Or "You're congested."

Then he stopped asking.

During the last month of his life a doctor told me every breath he took was like trying to breathe with an elephant standing on his chest. By then he'd moved into my sister's room. My grandmother was stuck in New York Hospital with her failed hip operation, and sick people often moved into our house. My mother knew how to make them comfortable. She knew what people needed and liked giving it to them. My bedroom shared a wall with two nervous breakdowns, one radical mastectomy, a divorce, my grandmother's hip, and my grandfather's lungs.

In November, when it wasn't too cold out, we'd sit on the patio. He'd turn his face to the sun, and I would take dictation. There were Morgen's recipes only he knew: Sauce Mousseline for the Brook Trout Stuffed with Fruits de Mer; Apple Fritters that accompanied the Jumbo Jersey Center-Cut Boneless Pork Chops. The secret in the Mashed Peas that went with the Extra-Thick Beef Tongue and Creamed Spinach. A high priority was Chopped Liver.

"The most important thing, darling, is you have to take the livers off the flame before they finish cooking. They have to still be pink inside. Off the flame, they continue cooking from their own heat. If you let them cook through in the skillet, they dry out. Take them off the flame when they're pink, and they'll stay moist. They won't overcook.

" *'Take off flame while still pink. . . .'*

"Then let them cool for fifteen minutes before adding the egg."

I check my recipe files. I can't find Morgen's Chopped Liver. I call my father.

"Dad? Do you remember Poppy's recipe for Chopped Liver?"

"How come every time a Jewish man gets a cold, a chicken has to die?" Dad says.

"Seriously, Dad."

"All right, Petroushka. Got a pencil? Take one chicken. Kill it. . . ."

Do you have any regrets?" I asked my grandfather a week before he went to the hospital for the last time. He was thoughtful. Then he answered, "I didn't buy the Carlyle during the Depression when I could have had it for a song. I let my accountant talk me out of buying 1450 Broadway when I could have had it for fifty thousand dollars. I didn't invest in Chock Full O'Nuts, because I was sure Americans would never put up with that kind of service. And I didn't buy Luchow's when they were giving it away."

He died ten days before I got married. I went to pick up what the hospital called his effects. A clerk handed me a clear plastic bag. In it were his long-sleeved yellow sweater, gray slacks, his Masonic ring, his wallet, and his bridge. In the wallet was his Social Security card, his Blue Cross/Blue Shield card, a twenty-four-year-old invitation to an elite New York bridge club my grandmother refused to let him join because other women would be there, a few singles, and one photograph. It was me, my high school graduation picture, a three-quarter view with a close-mouthed smile. I am gazing into nowhere. The white photographer's drape exposes my shoulders and crosses my breasts. I am wearing Cleopatra eyeliner, and my clavicles are sticking out. It was the fashion in my high school for seniors to have dozens of their graduation pictures printed. You'd autograph them for your friends to put in their wallets. Your popularity was measured by the fatness of your wallet and the length of the elastic you had to sew on the tab to get it to close. I don't for a minute think my grandfather carried the picture because I was special to him. Most likely I was the only person who ever thought to offer him a photo for his wallet. When I gave him the picture, he stared at it long and hard. Then he took the cigar out of his mouth and told me I was so thin and bony, I looked like a herring. The Herring Picture he called it. This I took as a compliment.

DAILY ⊚ NEWS

35¢   NEW YORK'S PICTURE NEWSPAPER®   Monday, August 13, 1990

DISARMING CHARM

JACK SMITH DAILY NEWS

BRAVE A plucky Ruth Wolko, 84, leaves Riverdale, Bronx, apartment yesterday after being held hostage for seven hours by a burglary suspect, who not only got a lecture about his choice of profession, but a nice kosher meal, too. See story on page 2

THE PVB's 18M LEMON

STORY ON PAGE 3

Aunt Ruthie makes the front page after hostage negotiators
exchange her for two cigarettes. (She never kept kosher.)

BUTTER COOKIES

Your Uncle Albert and I had a whirlpool romance," Aunt Ruthie tells me. Then she pauses. "Is that the word I mean?"

We're having lunch to celebrate her eighty-ninth birthday. She dabs a little applesauce on her blintzes.

"I make the best applesauce," she says. "You want to know the secret? I put in the pits."

"You leave them *in*?"

"There's taste in the pits," she explains. "You quarter the apples, cook them in water, then you put them through a . . . through a . . ." The word is gone.

There are 159,260 women in New York City over eighty. You see them taking tai chi at the Y. You see them at Fairway elbowing toward the Florida grapefruits or examining the string beans one by one. They're on the bus after ten and before three. In winter they wear woollies. You used to see them at the Women's Exchange and Mary Elizabeth's. You used to see them at Schrafft's having tuna on toasted cheese bread and hot fudge sundaes with coffee ice cream. New York's oldest women have outlived their hangouts. Most have outlived their husbands. One of them ran the marathon last year. Few are as lucky as Brooke Astor and Kitty Carlisle Hart and my mother's friend's mother Lola, who, at ninety-seven, stands on her dining-room table twice a year to clean the chandelier. What's a little old lady anymore anyway? Grace Paley? Matilda Krim? Aunt Ruthie?

"If I live to be a hundred, I won't finish these blintzes," Aunt Ruthie says. "Take one, darling."

"You really leave the pits in?"

"And the skin."

Maybe you've heard of my Aunt Ruthie. She's the woman who was taken hostage in her Bronx apartment by an ex-paratrooper on August 4, 1990. It was a hot night. She left her bathroom window open. José Cruz climbed in and held Aunt Ruthie at gunpoint for seven hours. BRAVE, the *Daily News* ran under her photo on page 1. YIDDISH CHARM NAILS SUSPECT, said the *New York Post*. He ate all her plums, a wedge of Jarlsberg, and three nectarines before the police exchanged her for two cigarettes.

"When you go to prison," Aunt Ruthie counseled him, "take out some books. Learn a different profession. It's important in life to get hold of yourself."

Aunt Ruthie got hold of herself young. After graduating Morris High, she got a clerical job at the Pathé Exchange on West Forty-fifth Street. Aunt Ruthie couldn't help noticing that the office supervisor, a Miss Maloubier, was taking lunch from twelve to four. Six months later Aunt Ruthie had Miss Maloubier's job. "I was so fast and thorough, they advanced me." She made fifty dollars a week, which she gave to her mother, who gave her an allowance. "That's the way it was then, darling. I didn't think anything else."

A woman who looks like George Burns sits down at the table next to us. She knows Aunt Ruthie from the building and starts complaining about the super, how he mops the lobby using the same bucket of water he uses to mop the basement, how she's been keeping an eye on him and she knows. When we finally disengage, Aunt Ruthie blinks at me in an exaggerated way. First one eye, then the other, then both, then one eye again. I think she is sending me a code that she doesn't like the woman, so I nod to show I get it. Then Aunt Ruthie tells me she can't see out of her left eye.

"You accept these things." She shrugs. "No pain, thank goodness."

Aunt Ruthie can remember the taste of her mother's egg sandwiches and recite "All the world's a stage." But she's puzzled she's "lost" Latin. In 1930, when she married Uncle Albert—"I was attracted to him. He was the Beau Brummel type"—her mother-in-law insisted she retire.

"But you'd worked there five years. You loved that job. Didn't you mind?"

"I ran sixteen girls in that office, but she was against it. *So* against it. At that time there weren't many married women working."

Aunt Ruthie's not tough, but she's resilient. She's what you'd call old New York genteel. I worry that when she dies, her syntax will disappear from the universe. There should be a place that preserves the way women spoke, the way the Yivo Institute preserves Yiddish. For instance, when you agree with Aunt Ruthie, she prolongs the agreement with "Am I right?" as in:

AUNT RUTHIE: So help me, that woman looks just like George Burns.
ME: You're right. She looks just like George Burns.
AUNT RUTHIE: Am I right?

"I'll be jiggered," she likes to say. "Out of this world." "Isn't it something?" "May I be struck with lightning." "Honest to God." "As I live and breathe." "She's not my cup of tea." "Mixed vegetables." "You should only never know." "I could eat her up." "Always the lady." "I won't hear of it." "Vichy." "Certainly." "Frigidaire" and "Down below" or "*There*."

Like the song says, she calls everybody "darling."

"Darling, do you think you could find this for me in a four-teen?"

"I'll have the toasted pimento cheese and a cup of coffee, dar-ling, if you don't mind."

"Darling, if you have a seat on the aisle, I'd be so appreciative."

And to me on the phone: "I had my hair done, darling. I wish you could see it."

I ask her about a word my grandmother used to use.

"*Umbashrign?* It's like God bless you. On that order, darling."

Aunt Ruthie lives by herself. She's not half of the New York Odd Couple, a widow and her live-in companion. You see these women on sunny days, walking with care or getting pushed. Aunt Ruthie does just fine, even though she was hit by a stolen van in front of Key Foods two years ago. She wound up with a broken hip and shoulder, and now, when she leaves the apart-ment, Aunt Ruthie uses a shopping cart for balance. She weights it with the Bronx Yellow Pages.

"I make out I'm going shopping." She laughs. In her black tight skirt, black sweater, and black heels with patent toe caps, Aunt Ruthie looks stylish even with the cart.

A friend stops by our table and admires her red jacket.

"Trying to get noticed, Ruth?"

"Well, what do you think?" Aunt Ruthie jokes back.

Then she whispers, "The *Blair Catalog*. Thirty-nine dollars," to me.

The three sisters—my grandmother Polly, Aunt Gertie, and Aunt Ruthie—all wound up having trouble walking. But it's especially sad to see Aunt Ruthie with a limp. She and Uncle Albert were the family dancers. At every fancy function they took over the dance floor, chin-flicking to the tango, kicking out to the cha-cha, fox-trotting so it actually looked like a trot, spin-ning in smiling synch, clearing the floor, everyone watching as Aunt Ruthie's fingers rested like the tip of a wing on Uncle Albert's palm, our very own Fred and Ginger.

Every week Aunt Ruthie gets together with the girls. These are new girls. The old girls, her four best friends, are dead. And every week Aunt Ruthie gets her pageboy done. It's still got a lot of black.

"Is that your real hair color?"

"I swear to you as my name is Ruth. But people don't believe me, so I tell them I use shoe polish."

Back at the apartment, Aunt Ruthie asks if I could use her mahjong set. When I admire a needlepoint pillow, she says, "Take it home." I follow her into the kitchen. There's Aunt Ruthie's twenty-four-inch white enamel gas stove, the one that's seen forty-three years of Chicken à la Thousand Island Dressing, Meat Loaf with Dole Pineapple Rings and Stuffed Cabbage with Ocean Spray Whole Cranberry Sauce, the vintage oven she uses for her butter cookies. The three sisters all made thumbprint butter cookies. They all used their mother's recipe, but the cookies came out different. Nana's were the roundest, Aunt Gertie's were the flattest, and Aunt Ruthie's were free-form. Nana's were the butteriest, Aunt Gertie's were the flakiest, and Aunt Ruthie's used the most sugar. Nana's were pale, Aunt Ruthie's were brown, and Aunt Gertie's shined because she alone painted the tops with egg white. The three sisters filled the thumbprint with jam or a chocolate morsel except for Aunt Gertie. In addition to jam and chocolate, Aunt Gertie improvised with walnut crumbs, although she was the only one who liked walnut crumbs. Sometimes Aunt Ruthie put a whole Hershey's Kiss in the thumbprint, creating a cookie of high promise. But the sorry fact is, her cookies were inedible. Each time Aunt Ruthie gave me a tin, I'd try one, hoping this batch would be different, that I'd be able to taste the butter and vanilla, that this time they'd be good. I'd take a bite, raise my eyebrows, and go "Ummm . . . UMMMMM!" because that's what Aunt Ruthie was waiting for. I'd smile and shake my head with faux wonder. Then I'd say, "They're so good. Can I save them for later?" How could I tell her they had freezer burn and left an oil slick on the roof of your mouth? Once I learned to cook, I knew what was wrong. Aunt Ruthie didn't use butter in her butter cookies. The Crisco must have been to save money.

Aunt Ruthie takes her carving knife out of a drawer. She unwraps a slice of marbled halvah from the birthday basket Mom sent from Zabar's. With decisiveness she cuts a piece. Then, wrapping it in waxed paper, "This is for your *husband,*" she warns in a different voice. "*You* don't need it."

I never anticipate the zinger. When I'm with Aunt Ruthie, I'm having such a good time I forget she does that. Even though I may not have spoken to Aunt Ruthie for two months because of a past zinger, all is forgotten when I am swept back into the culture of my youth, when I am called "darling," "light of my life," or her favorite, "my love." I am adored, adored. But then there it is—the Aunt Ruthie zinger. My heart and upper arms feel fizzy. It's an adrenaline surge, the kind you get crossing the street when a car almost clips you.

This is for your husband. You don't need it.

Zing! Does she think I'm fat? Zing! Zing! Was I going to scarf the slice on the Mosholu Parkway, allowing my husband to think I visited Aunt Ruthie without bringing something for him? That Aunt Ruthie provided no gift for the man of the house? Zing. Zing went the strings of my heart. What's the matter with me? Can't I have some halvah too?

It's a shocker, the Aunt Ruthie zinger. She loves you to death, she loves you so incredibly much you forget she zings. Then she zings. Sometimes I take a little vacation. I don't call. Then Aunt Ruthie phones, her voice wobbly, and says, "Why haven't I heard from you, my love?" and I'm overcome with missing her. Why does every encounter come with one poison dart? Is it the power to hurt that proves you still mean something to somebody? Is it a tic? Is this why the daughter-in-law I never met won't see her? Why the granddaughters don't call? Why has she never seen and held her great-grandchildren? How does Aunt Ruthie survive the hole in her heart where family should be?

"For the life of me"—Aunt Ruthie dabs her eyes with a hankie—"I don't know what I did. As God is my witness, you tell me, darling. What on the face of this earth did I do?"

This is the theme, the central gnawing conundrum of Aunt Ruthie's every waking day. How can people hate an old lady so much they won't let her see her own flesh and blood?

Some zings are breathtaking.

To a child having trouble in school: "Your brother gets nothing but straight A's. What a pity you're having such difficulties, darling."

To an aunt with a weight problem: "Would you like a safety pin for that seam, my love? Fat people are so hard on clothes."

To my mother whose hand-me-downs Aunt Ruthie depends on: "It cost me eleven fifty to fix the shoulders on the pink suit. Can you imagine, light of my life? Eleven dollars and fifty cents! It was that out of fashion."

To me as she points to one of my children: "Now *that* child is extraordinary."

What about the other one?

If you say, "Aunt Ruthie, it hurts my feelings you only inquire about one of my kids," her jaw drops open like a nutcracker. "Darling, you misunderstood me," she says.

Does she do it on purpose? Does she not know she does it? What's in it for her? Why does she keep doing the thing that makes what she wants most in life impossible? Only once, when my mother refused to retreat, did Aunt Ruthie back down. "I know." Aunt Ruthie wept. "I can't help myself. Forgive me, Audrey darling. I don't know why I do that."

I cherish Aunt Ruthie for loving my grandmother Polly as much as she did. "There's no words," Aunt Ruthie says. "I don't know how to describe her. She made up for everything heavy in my heart." And for remembering details like how my grandmother wore her braids on her wedding day and how a woman could fake having a hymen on her wedding night with chicken blood. Aunt Ruthie is the last survivor of the generation that spawned my mother. She never complains about money. She's never had any. She makes me think of my beloved godmother, whose financial security can't do a thing for her Alzheimer's. It's advanced to the stage where my dearest Dorothy doesn't know she's Dorothy. The last time I took her to lunch, she couldn't remember our names. We sat in a luncheonette on West Seventy-second Street, and she kept asking, ever polite because patterns of civility are the last thing to go, "Now, you are . . . ?" and "Who, may I ask, exactly are you?" The first few times I told her, "I'm Patty." Then I'd say, "I'm Patty. Cecil and Audrey's daughter, Jo Ann's sister, Peter and Polly's mother." Then I took a paper napkin out of the dispenser and began writing it down. Each time she asked me who I was, I'd write Patty on a napkin and hold it up for her to read. Then she'd work the clasp of her bag, stuff the napkin in, and say, "Ahhhh. And how do I get in touch with you . . . uh . . . Patty?" So I'd take the napkin back and write my phone number on it too. When we used up all the napkins in our dispenser, I took a dispenser from an empty table. Each time I wrote my name and number down, Dorothy looked relieved.

We walked back to her apartment at the Majestic, her handbag crammed with napkins. Then I left the city for the weekend. When I returned Sunday night, there were nineteen messages on my answering machine: "Hello. . . . Who are you?" "Hello. . . . Where are you?" "Hello. . . . Who is this?" "Hello. . . . Who is Patty?" "Hello, this is Patty. Call me." That was three years ago, when she was still able to speak. Aunt Ruthie is a reminder it doesn't have to be like that, not with our gene pool.

I thanked Aunt Ruthie for the needlepoint pillow and the halvah. "Good-bye, Aunt Ruthie." I bent to kiss her.

After visiting Aunt Ruthie, that night I dream I'm taking her to the Metropolitan Museum. "Leave your shopping cart at home," I tell her. "We'll slide." We do the Great Hall like ice-skaters, gliding over the stone floors in flat shoes.

I wake up thinking about her applesauce and call my mother.

"What's the thing you push food through that gets out the pits when you make applesauce?" I ask.

"A Foley Food Mill," Mom says.

So I dial the Bronx.

"Of course!" Aunt Ruthie gasps. "The letters are right there on the side! Darling, would you tell me something, please? I want to know. How on earth could I forget that?"

Ethel Edythe Shure Volk, the First National
Bank of Princeton's first calendar girl

With one or two notable exceptions everyone in our family was gorgeous. In a gorgeous family everybody looks like somebody else. That's how you establish how gorgeous they are. My mother was a Lana Turner double. My father bore an uncanny resemblance to Stewart Granger *and* Prince Philip—people actually took sides. My mother's mother was a Gloria Swanson look-alike. My sister was likened to two people: Elizabeth Taylor and Cyd Charisse. That left me.

"So who do you think she takes after?"

"I don't know. Lily Pons?"

Lily Pons? Who was Lily Pons? How come everybody else looked like a brand name, and I looked like Lily Pons? Whoever Lily Pons was, she must have had gorgeous arms. One day, while my grandmother was playing canasta with her sisters, I stood in her kitchen making a ham sandwich.

"Look at that arm." She glanced up from the card table.

"Did you ever in your life see such an arm?" Aunt Ruthie chimed in.

"As God is my witness," Aunt Gertie swore, "never."

NANA: "Look how it curves near the shoulder!"

RUTHIE: "Look how it moves!"

GERTIE: "Gorgeous!"

NANA: "Did you ever?"

GERTIE and RUTHIE: "Never!"

In a gorgeous family even *meat* can be gorgeous. As in, "That's a gorgeous lamb chop."

Objects too.

"Is that a gorgeous hat or what?"

"Did you ever?"

"May I be struck with lightning, never."

My father set the standard for men. Tall, skinny, with a big nose and plummy lips, he was our male gorgeousness ideal. Naturally, my sister and I married tall, skinny men with big noses and plummy lips. Her husband looks like Montgomery Clift. Mine, like Gregory Peck.

In a gorgeous family, whatever you have, it's gorgeous. If it's on the small size, it's "petite." If it's bigger than normal, it's "generous." Take our feet. Most of us had generous ones.

"What a shame." Relatives would point out an otherwise nice-looking person. "Look how shrimpy her feet are."

We were told large feet made us look more balanced. We were less likely to tip over. Big-foot support arrived via Jackie Kennedy. My sister, who by the time she was eleven was taller than our mother, had the biggest feet of all. How I longed for them. With nine and a halfs, I felt like a munchkin. I couldn't wait to get pregnant and add half a size. If hair was kinky, it was naturally curly. If hair was limp, it was Garboesque.

In the beginning I hoped I was gorgeous too. If commenting on someone's looks was the first thing people did when they ran into each other, gorgeousness had to be important. "Muh-wah! Muh-wah!" They'd air kiss. "You look gorgeous!"

Every chance meeting started with a mention of looks. Every parting was followed by a looks postmortem. But all this time something nagged at me: What did *I* have to do with how I looked? Wasn't being gorgeous a genetic fluke, like being able to roll your tongue or make your thumb touch your wrist? It wasn't something you could take credit for like cleaning your plate.

When I was twelve, we moved to Kings Point, one of nine villages forming a town called Great Neck. It was a suburb where girls got their hair done every Saturday. On Saturdays I'd feel gorgeous too. Was I only as good as my do? I loathed how important it was to have the single solitary look that passed for beauty. I couldn't bear having my looks be the barometer of my soul. The only time I ever heard my mother curse was when she broke a fingernail. I decided I would never have long nails. Watching her apply pancake makeup to her gorgeous face with a clammy beige sponge that smelled like an attic, I swore I'd never wear any of that stuff either. If artifice was the hallmark of beauty, how legitimate was beauty? My mother didn't need makeup. She was more gorgeous without it. I thought she was the most beautiful woman in the world. She took this in her stride. If pressed, she would say Ingrid Bergman was the most beautiful woman in the world. Despite "a low hairline," my grandmother voted for Kay Francis.

I decided not to let looks be important. And they weren't until I had the occasion to doubt mine. One summer at camp a bunk bitch put together the perfect girl:

"Bonnie's knees . . ." Harriet made a list. "Sue's nose . . . Addie's hair . . . Diane's waist . . ." Nothing came from me.

"Of course you're gorgeous," my mother consoled me. "Anytime someone tries to hurt you, it's because they're jealous."

It was self-preservation. I had to make gorgeous not matter. If I was gorgeous, fine. If I wasn't, that was okay too. Gorgeous was too frivolous an arena to compete in. I began loathing compliments.

"Big deal," I'd respond. "Cut to the chase." Or "My skin is so smooth? What were you expecting? Pumice?"

I especially couldn't stand the three questions my mother never failed to ask after a party: "How did you look? What did you wear? Were you the most gorgeous girl there?"

Most of all I detested the possibility that people were saying I was gorgeous to make me feel good. And the dark thing that meant was that maybe, just maybe, I wasn't gorgeous after all. That compliments were good manners, like "Let's have lunch" or "Nice to meet you." If I was so gorgeous, how come the most gorgeous boy in our high school never asked me out? How come nobody outside the family ever gasped and said, "Is she gorgeous or what?"

"Jewish girls don't hit their stride till their thirties," my mother consoled me. "Gentile girls peak before twenty."

Always, the first day of school, I would check out all the other mothers. There was never any competition. Mine was the most gorgeous.

"Did anyone ever tell you you have one gorgeous mother?" was the refrain of my youth.

"Your mother? Go on. I thought she was your sister!"

"Do you know," strangers would say as if I didn't know, as if it was news, "your mother really is quite beautiful."

"Thank you." My mother's eyes would widen as if she'd never heard it before.

Sundays, when the family sat down to breakfast together, my father would say, "Isn't your mother the most gorgeous woman in the world?"

"Yes!" my sister and I would answer—glad she was, sorry we weren't.

People looked at me with curiosity. "Tell me," they'd ask. "What's it like to have such a gorgeous mother?"

To support the idea that gorgeousness didn't matter, I began to collect women I admired who, by the gorgeous family's standards, weren't gorgeous: Gertrude Stein, Emily Dickinson, Alice Neel, Ella Fitzgerald, Flannery O'Connor, Simone de Beauvoir. Then a funny thing happened. They got gorgeous.

Loving them transformed them. In college there was an odd-looking boy in my drawing class. David had a potbelly. His acne raged. But he was funny and quirky and a brilliant renderer. After class I'd hang around his easel to see what he'd done. We began to take walks. I started thinking his skin wasn't so bad and the fact that it fulminated was a sign of masculinity, a testosterone zetz. David became even more attractive because he didn't seem to care if he was.

One afternoon, lying in the grass between classes, bodies almost touching, we stared at the sky. "David," I leaned over him, "have you ever wanted to kiss me?"

"No," he said.

Mostly though, I was attracted to gorgeous men. I couldn't help myself. They didn't have to be 100 percent gorgeous, but inky hair, rosy cheeks, a well-defined platysma popping out of a white T-shirt, bulging forearm veins, or the one that still takes my breath away—a concave spinal column, the kind of spine that goes in, a valley in the mountains of a man's back. Any one of those and I was powerless. Yes, I loved how they looked. But I had a double standard. I resented that what may have drawn them to me had anything at all to do with how I looked.

I lived in a whirl of beauty. But even a gorgeous family has degrees. My mother was a true beauty. Her mother was a classic beauty. But it was my father's mother, Ethel Edythe Shure Volk Wolf, who was considered a *great* beauty. Her thick chestnut hair was long enough to sit on. It had to be professionally combed. Her eyes were light blue and her nose was tiny. Granny Ethel was so gorgeous, she once received a letter addressed simply:

Post, postman
Do your duty
Deliver this letter
To the Princeton beauty

There was one unusual aspect to Granny's gorgeousness. It had what some people might call a tragic flaw. No one else I knew with this flaw was considered gorgeous. But the rest of Granny's beauty was of such magnitude, it overrode the problem. She was—there's no other word for it—fat. Not plump. Not zaftig. Fat.

"She was made when meat was cheap," Dad used to say when he saw a fat woman. "It must be jelly 'cause jam don't shake like that!" or "Fat, fat, the water rat. Forty bullets in your hat." But never about his mother.

"It was more than fat," my sister says now. "She had no muscle tone."

Exercise in my grandmother's day meant walking two blocks on Sunday to pick up bagels. Granny's upper arms hung. Six grandchildren used them as pillows. You could flick the upper part, and it would swing until somebody quieted their palms on either side to make it stop. Those arms held the secret of perpetual motion. We pressed our cheeks into their warm powdered softness. She laughed.

G ranny Ethel was on an eternal diet. When we ate in restaurants, she'd work the breadbasket, starting with the Ry-Krisp because she was watching her weight. When those were gone, she'd dive into the saltines followed by the sesame breadsticks. Only then, if the appetizer still hadn't arrived, if the waiter wasn't in sight, if there was still downtime, would she go through the salt sticks and rolls: kaiser, Parker House, poppy seed, working her way up calorically to the hot cross buns.

When I was five, Granny took me to Schrafft's to introduce

me to the ice-cream soda. We sat at the polished mahogany counter, and she ordered me a white-and-black, a vanilla soda with chocolate ice cream. Then in her amused and patient way she taught me how to drink through a straw: "Pretend your mouth is an Electrolux." It worked. That ice-cream soda was the best thing I'd tasted to date, cold and sweet to drink, cold and sweet to eat. And then there was the taste, the classic chocolate and vanilla, a combination that remains unparalleled. I dangled my legs from the stool hoping that soda never would end.

When Granny married her second husband, Charles Wolf, she left Manhattan and bought a house in Trenton. Then they bought a winter home in Miami, where they maintained a cabana at the Thunderbird. From the time I was eight, I would be sent to visit them at Christmas. Dad would wrap a sturgeon in waxed paper and two layers of gold foil, and I would sit on the plane with the sturgeon on my lap. The Flying Fish I called it. Planes to Florida took six hours then. Men wore suits, and women wore white gloves to fly. There were propellers out the window. I would sit on the plane for six hours holding the sturgeon. When the plane landed, I'd scan the crowd on the tarmac. Granny would be there making a visor out of her hand. Then she'd spot me and wave. I would see her eyes roam until they lit on the sturgeon. The relief, the joy, on her face. The question for me was, Who was she happiest to see?

Granny's house wasn't big. To get to the guest bathroom, I had to pass the kitchen. And there she'd be, night after night, standing at the counter, picking at the sturgeon. She'd be in an enormous belted robe, her hair in a loose thick braid down her back. She went through the fish in layers. First she'd eat it by the slice. Then she'd scavenge the debris. Finally she'd peck the skin. Toward the end of my week in Florida, the sturgeon remains were wrapped in newspaper and I'd go home. Only Granny ate the sturgeon. When friends stopped by, she put out mixed nuts and mosaics of dried fruit on wicker trays. These arrangements came packaged with an ivory-toned two-pronged plastic fork. But Granny preferred her own dried fruit instruments, an engraved silver nutcracker with a matching metal pick. Some of the things—the dried apricots and glazed maraschino cherries—were identifiable. But some were mysterious, beige with veins, black with stubble.

Jacob Volk had been Orthodox. Charles Wolf was merely kosher. Granny practiced no religion, but the problem, even though she kept a kosher home for Charles, was that she loved Chinese food. I always knew when she was going to take me for Chinese because she'd start the conversation with, "Don't tell Grandpa Charles." Then we'd slink to the kind of Chinese restaurant where it always looks like night. Granny would check the street to make sure no one she knew saw us going in. She'd order Chop Suey, Chow Mein, and Almond Char Sue Ding. When the New York branch of the family ate Chinese, we were more adventurous: Moo Goo Gai Pan and War Hoo Hip Har. What we ordered didn't need gray cornstarch to hold it together. Still, Granny savored every bite. She ate with elegance and the kind of resolve that said, "This is hard work, this business of eating. I am, however, up to the task." Afterward she would drink seltzer to "aid digestion."

I liked Grandpa Charles. He was gentle, and even when children spoke, he listened as if he were interested. I was proud of him for inventing the toothless plastic zipper. He gave me handbags he manufactured under the name Park Lane and laughed when I tickled his feet. Once, he took me on a tour of his tannery in New Jersey. It was a sunny, Santa's workshop sort of place, sunken tubs filled with hides and men in brown leather aprons working at tables with hammers and awls. I loved his accent. When he said, "So, Ettel, tell me vot. Vair you took da kinder fair loonch?" I'd let Granny answer. "Wolfie's." She'd lie. Or "Pickin' Chicken, Charles."

In Florida we ate out most nights. When Granny did cook, it was a broiled piece of meat and the salad she invented—a mound of shredded carrots moistened with V-8 juice. That salad had everything: the bright orange carrots, the lacquer of red juice. The sweet, the sour. The crunchy, the wet. I would sit alone by the window at her kitchen table and chew it, watching two great beams of light cross and part from each other in the black night sky. I didn't ask her what the lights were for. I knew. They were to detect enemy planes so the army could shoot them down before they shot us. It never occurred to me the lights were from the airport and we weren't at war. Anything was possible in Florida. To a New York girl of eight, Florida wasn't really America. The buses, water fountains, and bathrooms were segregated.

You look like you lost weight," people would say to Granny when they ran into her. But she hadn't. She just went up, up, up, a woman who couldn't say no to a fine mouthful, who saw the potential to make every bite the best. When she came to the store, she'd start out French with the *Filet de Truite au Sauce Mousseline* my father had the chef run under the salamander. She would eat the delicate fish with just the right amount of creamy bronzed sauce on each forkful. Then she'd whiz to Warsaw for the Chopped Chicken Livers with Chicken Fat, which she'd meticulously spread to the corners of her toast. Then back to France via Spain for her favorite soup, Jellied Madrilène, a cold consommé flavored with fresh tomato juice and served with a slice of lemon. "For protein" Granny traveled to China and the White Peking Duck with Coconutted Sweet Potatoes. She gnawed bones with delicacy. Like my father, she worked them over, brittled them good, scranching and craunching, and when they were stark gray and gristle-free, she'd eye the bones on other people's plates and say, "You're not leaving those, are you?"

October 26 was Granny Ethel's birthday, and on the closest

Saturday to it, she'd throw herself a party. All six grandchildren, their parents, and a herd of friends and relatives took over the Terrace Room of the Hotel New Yorker on Eighth Avenue and Thirty-fourth Street. There would be a floor show. We could order anything we wanted. The orchestra would strike up "Happy Birthday" as a cake was wheeled in. Then the master of ceremonies would invite anyone who wanted to perform up to the microphone. My sister and I were the only ones that went. Every year we'd get up and sing the same song: "Take Me Out to the Ball Game." And every year we'd bring the house down by substituting the word "Yankees" for "home team" in the last verse:

> For it's root, root, root for the Yankees
> If they don't win it's a shame
> For it's one, two, three strikes you're out
> ` At the old ball game!

In 1976 the Hotel New Yorker was sold to the Moonies, but until then it was the largest hotel in New York, with twenty-five hundred rooms, thirty-five chefs, and twenty full-time manicurists.

G ranny wore a corset called an all-in-one. It included a bra, waist cincher with stays, and knee-length girdle. Satin ribbons hid the garters. It was engineered with reinforced seams. The all-in-one pressed everything in so tight her back was pleated. Granny preferred to have her clothes made. At my sister's wedding she wore a blue lace dress that matched her eyes. And on her head, a tiny blue pillbox with a blue dotted veil. Her wrists were loaded with bracelets, ropes of pearls looped her neck. Later that evening one of my mother's friends who'd never met Granny before said, "That's the woman you told me was so gorgeous? She's not gorgeous. Audrey, she's old and she's fat." Mom told me this in disbelief. I was shocked too. Granny was a great beauty. All of us knew that. But when I look at the pictures of her in my sister's wedding album now, it's possible to see her without myth.

The older Granny got, the whiter her long hair was at the crown. But the ends of it stayed chestnut. That hair dated her like the rings of a tree. I liked to think Jacob Volk had known those ends, that he had touched the chestnut part, that I was seeing hair he had seen.

That picture in my sister's wedding album turned out to be Granny's last. She died in what was then called Doctor's Hospital on East End Avenue. Cancer of the bladder. The family story was that before she married Charles, she'd flown to Washington for an abortion and the doctor nicked her bladder. That resulted in a condition that forced her to go to the urologist twice a week to get her bladder pumped. She believed this is what gave her cancer. Everyone who gets cancer thinks they know why. Maybe she was right. I don't know. I do know that when she got slim, it was the way no one wants to get slim. It broke our hearts to see her lose her appetite. Sturgeon sandwiches withered on her bed tray. Ice-cream sodas warmed and went flat. Tea was too much. "Ethel, you lost weight!" Friends tried to cheer her when they visited, but that was no longer what she yearned to hear.

My father was powerless. He'd stand over her bed and say "Mother? Mother?" She'd roll her head and groan. There was nothing anybody could do.

"Promise me something," he said while we waited for a cab in front of the hospital.

"What?"

"If I'm ever suffering like that, promise me you'll kill me."

"I could never do that."

"There's nothing to it. You inject an air bubble between my toes. The coroner will never find it."

"I couldn't do that, Dad."

"You have to, Patricia Gay. Promise me."

"Okay."

I swore to myself that if I ever had a daughter, I'd make sure she wasn't tyrannized by beauty. Life would be different for her. She would never wonder, Am I gorgeous? Not because she was or wasn't, but because it wouldn't matter. I'd devalue gorgeous. Gorgeous would be a fact of life, a nonadvantage. Brains, wit, drive, and kindness, waking up every morning wondering, What's next?—who needs gorgeous if you've got all that? Gorgeous would be neither a plus nor a minus, just there, like the Great Barrier Reef. My girlchik would never have good days or bad days based on makeup. She'd never enter a room less confident thanks to her hair. Beauty would be a nonissue. The plan was simple: If I never told her she looked good, she'd never wonder if she looked bad.

Then I had a daughter. A daughter!

"Look!" I showed my husband her toes in the delivery room. "They're like fringe! Did you ever in your life see anything so gorgeous?"

Everyone who came to the apartment saw the toes. They were all the same length, straight and perfectly shaped. "Aren't they like little pink piano keys?" I said to everyone. "Doesn't she look like a Sarah Bernhardt peony? Did you ever see anything so pink?" I praised her earlobes and her navel. I praised her ankles and her chin. Her nostrils, her dark eyes, her thighs. I was out of control, couldn't help myself. What difference did it make? She couldn't understand. I called her Polly after my Gloria Swanson-ish grandmother. I allowed myself to revel in her beauty. I told myself when she started to speak, I'd stop. Then I couldn't. She was too gorgeous. To test my objectivity, I invented the Looking Game. I still play it. When Polly's back is turned, I say to myself: I am looking at this person for the first time. What do I think? And then, when she turns around, I look at her as if she's a stranger, as if I've never seen that face in my life and am forming a first impression. Always I am struck by her gorgeousness. It never fails. And along with this observation comes a great, dam-breaking, mother-lode flood of love. It's the gorgeous-love connection, the gorgeous-love one-two. And it was realizing this recently that suddenly I understood: Gorgeousness in my family is love. Saying "You are gorgeous" is saying "I love you." To love someone, no matter what they look like, is to see them as beautiful.

I don't love my children because they're gorgeous, even if they're gorgeous because I love them.

Ettie Volk Stavin, a self-styled pioneer
in marriage and family therapy

Over time in a family anything is possible. Fourteen years after Jacob Volk's sisters tried to steal his children from Granny Ethel, she forgave one of them. Ethel and Aunt Ettie became best friends. They requested that when they died they be buried side by side, each with a deck of cards so they could play in the afterlife. Ettie and Ethel loved this idea. But two years after Ethel died, Aunt Harriet dug her up, and Granny settled down permanently in her daughter's plot.

Aunt Ettie had thick blond hair that looked blown back by a cyclotron. She had the long Volk nose that dips into your mouth when you laugh. Her bearing was regal. Her breasts were heroic. Once when we were sharing the back seat of a car, her beads broke. I started scrambling on the floor. "Don't worry," she said. "My bosoms are so big, they'll catch them."

She dressed in layers of black scarves and chiffon. She was heavyset, but all this filmy cloth gave her the appearance of fluttering. You knew when she entered a room. Nine months a year, she draped five sables around her neck, each one biting the tail of the one in front. Most of the time she looked as if she were about to have tea with a European expatriate who'd lost his title in a revolution. Sometimes she was.

If Granny had me for an afternoon but found something else to do, she'd drop me off at Aunt Ettie's. Aunt Ettie didn't have food for kids, but she could always scare up a few Lorna Doones. We had the Classics Illustrated *Lorna Doone* by Richard Doddridge Blackmore. Dad came home one Saturday with the first 103 issues, his way of exposing us to literature. We would read the Classics and get hooked. We'd segue from comics to the real thing. Charles Dickens, Edgar Allan Poe, Bret Harte, Victor Hugo, Mark Twain, Harriet Beecher Stowe, Herman Melville, Charlotte Brontë, Sir Arthur Conan Doyle. *Lorna Doone* was one of my favorites. But I failed to see how a captive seventeenth-century English maiden from windswept Exmoor related to the cookie. Lorna Doones were good. They were buttery and unpretentious, a poor man's shortbread. You could nibble them around the raised Lorna Doone logo and make it interesting. Aunt Ettie would give me three on a plate and a glass of milk. Then she'd sit across the table in her subway-tiled kitchen on West Eighty-sixth Street and drink tea out of a glass with cherry preserves on the bottom.

Aunt Ettie had three sons. Cecil studied philosophy at N.Y.U. Maurice became a dentist, like his father. And Steve hopped freight cars and went around the country with a program called the CCC developed by Roosevelt to employ people during the Depression. Aunt Ettie made me laugh. But the reason I liked being around her was she had a quality I attributed to men. She was direct. There was no subtext. You didn't have to worry about double meanings. She was easy to talk to. She'd seen and done so much, she didn't pass judgment. Aunt Ettie was emotionally streamlined. Passing through water, she would cause the least disturbance.

Because Aunt Ettie liked to travel, she kept a packed steamer trunk in her hallway at all times. She had a deal with the *Bergens-fjord*. If a stateroom was still available or if someone canceled at the last minute, she could have it at half price. She could be at the pier in thirty minutes.

Every year Ettie went around the world on the *Bergensfjord*. She went to London. She went to the Pyramids. She went to zee Kasbah. And when she came back, she came back with stories. Once she sailed with the Duke and Duchess of Windsor. "What are they like?" We couldn't wait to know. She laughed and told us, "At night the Duke dresses up like a girl!" Was it a costume party? Did she see him in his kilt? Was the Duke a cross-dresser? Once, a woman's husband died mid-Atlantic, and "they kept him on ice" because his wife was in a bridge tournament and couldn't let her partner down. Aunt Ettie wore costume jewelry on these cruises. She didn't want to worry about her good stuff. "On me they think it's real," she'd say. She carried a black sack filled with coins, modeling herself on John D. Rockefeller, who used to give away dimes. "I tip everybody," Aunt Ettie said. "And everybody likes me."

She was worldly in another way too. She separated twice from her husband Nathan, the dentist. After Nathan died, she met Mr. Weiss on a cruise and married him. She was attracted to the idea that Mr. Weiss wanted them to be married yet independent. She thought that was forward-thinking. But what independent wound up meaning was that Mr. Weiss wanted to go Dutch. Ettie divorced him.

Separation was unusual at the time. Divorce was unheard of. This gave Aunt Ettie a strange kind of elevated status. Her advice on love matters became hotly sought. Who knows better how to save a marriage than someone who's loused up two? Ettie knew things other women could only guess at. She had a fresh vantage point on the complexities of human nature. She understood what were then called *drives*. I thought of Aunt Ettie as the Colette of the Upper West Side.

She had lots of friends. Her apartment was big. She had several regular card games, and afterward she'd serve blackberry brandy. A recurrent theme began to surface. A friend would stay late, and sitting on Aunt Ettie's horsehair love seat, she'd have another brandy. Then she'd reach for the tissues on a Moroccan tray and say, "Ettie. My husband—I think he's philandering. What am I going to do?"

The first question Ettie asked was always the same: "Do you want him?" (Aunt Ettie told me once that she was the only woman she knew who didn't want two men.)

"*Yeeeeeeeeeeeeees*," her friend would say.

That's when Aunt Ettie would reveal her Orchid Trick.

"First, send yourself an orchid," she'd begin. "Leave it in the icebox. Put on your best dress. Go out before he gets home. I don't care where you go. Go to the movies, go someplace, sit on a bench, but go. When your husband comes home and looks in the icebox, he'll see the orchid. Then he'll wonder, Why is there an orchid in the icebox? Next he'll wonder, Who gave her the orchid? Get home very late. He will have been sitting up in the window waiting for you. He'll be watching through the blinds and stewing. Take a long time getting out of the cab. When you get to the bedroom, he'll be in bed pretending to be asleep. Hum lightly under your breath. Sigh a few times while you get undressed. Make it obvious, though, that you're trying hard not to wake him up. He will not dare ask you where the orchid came from or where you were. A guilty man never dares to ask. Leave orchids in the icebox a few more times. Act happy. You probably won't need to spend the night out again."

Aunt Ettie said the Orchid Trick never failed. She'd invented it for herself and said it "rekindled the flame." I like to imagine her leaning into her fridge with a stripe of light bouncing off the glass eyes of her sables, placing a purple cattleya in a clear plastic box next to some farmer cheese. It wouldn't surprise me if she'd tucked a card in too: "For my darling Ettie, Thank you for last night." Or "Ettie, 'A lute whose lending chord is gone is what I am without you.'" Or "Sweetheart, your emerald eyes have pierced my heart."

My sister was the first one from our generation to have a baby. We took Aunt Ettie to meet her great-great-niece Elizabeth. Ettie held the baby and said, "She's named after a queen, and she holds her head nobly like a queen." Actually, Elizabeth wasn't named after Queen Elizabeth at all. She was named after Ettie's best friend, Granny Ethel. But "holding her head nobly like a queen" was a fresh compliment. And from then on, whenever we held Elizabeth or talked about her, we'd say, "Doesn't she hold her head nobly like a queen?"

Lana Turner and Gloria Swanson get ready for a party.

CHOPPED EGG

Thursday was Mattie's night off and when we lived in New York, since my mother didn't cook, we'd eat at my grandmother's. Then we moved to the suburbs and that was too long a drive. So we'd take the car to Shantung in that precursor of the Banana-Sonoma mall, the local shopping center. Mom would order a Sidecar, an amber cocktail made with brandy, Triple Sec, and lemon juice, and we'd start with ribs.

But as my sister and I grew diet-conscious, Thursday night dinner shifted to North Shore Steak House on Northern Boulevard. Restaurant families tip everyone. They tip well. They know firsthand how hard the work is and how often customers under-tip. Even when the service is rotten, restaurant families overtip. In addition to the waiter, they tip the captain, the maître d', and always the most neglected person—the one who, if he does the job right, is invisible, the one who works hardest for least—the astonished busboy who'd sometimes bow when Dad pressed two dollars in his hand.

There's a heightened alertness, ions get cranked when restaurant people walk into a restaurant. Restaurant people instinctively recognize each other. At North Shore we'd get the best table (you can see everybody, everybody can see you, not near the kitchen, the entrance or the powder rooms) and the best waiter, Jim, who nodded his head when we ordered and said, "Very good, Mrs. Volk." When we ate out with Dad, we'd tell him what we wanted and he would speak to the waiter: "My wife will have . . . My eldest daughter would like . . ." But when no man was present, we ordered individually. Mom had the pork chops with applesauce, my sister and I, the sliced steak. The house salad, iceberg tossed with Romaine, was sixties predictable. It was the dressing that set it apart. White, acidic, garlicky, and full of Dijon mustard, it didn't slide off the leaves. It was clingy and piquant. Piquant is too rare a sensation in food. For echt piquancy, nothing can touch the Welsh rarebit sandwich at the counter of the Fountain Restaurant in Fortnum & Mason with its molten Day-Glo cheese. Listed on the menu under Toasted and Savory it is extreme piquancy, involving everything in the oral cavity in a head-on collision. The tongue curls. The palate throbs. The gums hum. You feel it in your teeth.

I was sixteen the day I came home from school and found Mom in the kitchen. She'd never made dinner except for Sunday bacon and eggs. But there she was lifting lids, sniffing, stirring. She'd tied one of Mattie's white aprons over her Gino Paoli knit suit that would someday be mine.

"I'm making dinner!" she said. "Wash your hands! It's almost six!"

No matter what was going on in our lives, we sat down to the table at six. Watches were synchronized. One minute late was not tolerated. You had to be in your seat with your napkin in your lap at six *exactly*. That was when the food was so hot it still sizzled. That was when it was timed to be served. No one could start eating until everyone was seated. If you weren't at the table at six on the dot, people would have to wait for you. Keeping hungry people waiting for food was unforgivable. Treating Mattie's labor with indifference was unforgivable too. No one should have to eat cold food just because *you* lost track of time playing strip poker in your boyfriend's basement.

"What are you making?" I asked my mother.

"Veal Stroganoff," she said.

At six we congregated in the breakfast room. Mom carried in the silver well and tree. The well and tree, a wedding present from Aunt Gertie, had three parts. The wells on the sides cradled side dishes—the vegetables and starches. The concave tree in the center was for the main course. Whenever my father sliced steak or roast beef and put it in the tree, the juices ran down the concave branches and puddled in the root ball. He would soak them up with bread, then feed some to my sister and me. It was hot, blood-soaked white bread, softer than cotton candy. When Dad carved, he stemmed drips off the carving board with white bread dams. Those we ate too. *Jus lie* was good for you. It "built you up." My friend Steve's mother used to juice raw steak for him. He started every day with a glass of blood.

Mom stood at my left with the well and tree. I tonged some beans on my plate, spooned a little rice, then covered it with the Stroganoff. It was a creamy café-au-lait color.

My sister helped herself, then filled Mom's plate. When she returned from the kitchen, Mom brandished her napkin and we dug in. I stabbed a strip of the veal. I put it in my mouth. I looked sideways at my sister. She was looking at me. There was no way we could swallow it. Something was terribly wrong.

I pressed my napkin to my lips. The only taste in the world, besides medicine, the only *food* taste I couldn't stand, that even the thought of made me gag, was licorice. Licorice meat?

"What are you *doing*?" Mom said.

"Taste it."

She took a bite.

"My God!" she said.

In the kitchen, she reread the recipe. She checked the spices and sniffed the sour cream. "I don't know what it could be, girls," she said. Then she examined the bottle of white wine she'd grabbed to stew the meat in.

RICARD ANISETTE, the label read.

We headed for North Shore. Over steak and pork chops, we laughed about Mom's *Veau Ricard*. She didn't cook dinner again for thirty years.

Now I love her cooking. Like all things Mom decides to do (taking up tennis in her forties, then whipping me, going for a master's degree at sixty-four), she does it with style and commitment. She researches. My favorite dishes are Aunt Renee Birns's Chicken Curry and Mrs. Brill's Cabbage Soup. No one can make a burger as crusty on the outside and rosy on the inside as she can. My mother is a world-class *searer*. She seals the juices in a fragile carapace of carbon. She can *hear* when the pan is ready. Her chopped egg is her brother's favorite food in the world.

"Darling," he says, thrilled, "you made this for *me*?"

She mounds it in the caviar server, then circles it with Ritz crackers. "All for you, Bob."

He eats it up, piling the crackers high. Years later, when he'd lost his sense of taste, he'd eat it anyway, loving it from memory. "Audrey darling, this is terrific," he'd say.

Mom's trick with chopped egg is chopping the mayonnaise and salt into the eggs *while they're still warm* using a double-bladed mezzaluna *in a wooden cutting bowl*. She doesn't overchop, so the whites are still squeaky. Don't bother making Mom's chopped egg if you're going to practically purée it or chop it in a Pyrex bowl. It won't taste the same. Do microscopic bits of wood get into the egg? Does ancient mayonnaise leech out from the wood?

Whenever we went to Long Beach, she'd make chopped egg sandwiches and wrap them in waxed paper. The eggy mayo would soak into the warming Wonder Bread and turn it yellow. But the real taste of Long Beach was a hot dog at the Roadside Rest. Or a sloppy, flappy burger piled high with mayonnaisey

slaw and a slab of tomato at the Texas Ranger. I've tried to dupli-
cate the taste of a Rangeburger, but you need a greasy griddle
and it's hard to find meat that cheap.

I started going to Long Beach the July I was born. My parents
would rent a house, and my grandparents would rent one next
door. Then my great-grandparents would move in with them. In
summer we duplicated our four-generation Manhattan Diaspora
by the Atlantic. I would sleep under mosquito netting and watch
the light stream through the swirling dots of dust. I would pour
orange juice into my milk and cereal and pretend it was a
Creamsicle.

In Long Beach what we ate still came from the store. Not that
we ate the prepared food, good as it was. Restaurant families
rarely do. They have their own tastes. Homemade recipes are too
labor-intensive for a popular restaurant. No good chef has the
time to cook everything *à la minute.*

Morgen's kind of kitchen has vanished. Santos, the head chef,
could make anything. The trend in fusion cooking today com-
bines two cuisines. Santos kept his cultures pure. He cooked
what was called a continental menu. Each foreign dish was made
strictly the way it was made in its country of origin. The inven-
tiveness came from the inventory, the repertoire, how many
main courses you could make and what would accompany
them. There were the usual Diamond Jim Brady prime ribs,
steaks, chops, and seafood. Customers counted on standbys. But
Morgen's was also the United Nations of food. The dinner menu
from Wednesday, June 3, 1981, lists eighteen foreign specialties
of the day plus the usual thirty-six entrées. Vichyssoise was on
tap. Polynesian Chicken with Javanese Coconut. Duckling
Montmorency, Swedish Salmon in Aspic with Mustard Sauce,
Steak à la Deutsch, Veal Piccata, Shish Kebab à la Turque, Calves
Liver Veneziana with Noodles Sienna, Curried Scallops with
Rajah Rice, Fillet of Sole au Fruits de Mer, a giant, unfinishable
slab of mittel-European meat called Gedampte Rinderbrust, and
my all-time favorite menu listing, unleashing the virtuosity of his

menu muse, Dad's take on chicken soup: Essence of Young Fowl with Matzo Dumpling.

We love *savoureux*—food with plenty of taste. We appreciate subtlety, but we like to spring a food's energy. The difference between salt added before cooking, during cooking, and after cooking is oceanic. The difference between *salts*. We tune food. Just because something's good, doesn't mean more of it is better. All cooking is a pas de deux between complements and contrasts. How do you wring the most out of a radish? How do you fry an egg so the border is crackling brown lace? What does sugar do for tomatoes? How much vinegar do you add to the honey so it tastes more like honey than honey without vinegar?

My mother was home for dinner, but four lunches a week she was on the floor, working the line. She and Dad were a team. Mom, the elegant beauty in the fabulous Donald Brooks, Geoffrey Beene, or Bill Blass for Maurice Rentner. Dad, Clyde Beatty in the center ring. They orchestrated fifty tables, the bar, 194 customers, 16 waiters, 16 busboys, 1 captain, 1 manager, the hatcheck girl, and Miss Carlotta, the riveled attendant in the ladies' room. At lunch, when the place was rocking, they used a code of hand signals to signify "Get a busboy to clear the deuce at six!", "Table twelve needs a check!" Or Mom would raise three fingers above the crowd, and Dad would raise three back if he had a "three" and she'd release the next clot of customers from behind a red velvet rope.

No matter how long the line was, Mom would say, "Only five minutes!" when customers asked about the wait. And because she was so glamorous, so charming, people rarely grouched when it stretched to thirty. Turnover was key. If lunch went from 11:30 to 3:00, you could turn a table three, sometimes four times. Saturdays, after he'd closed the books, Dad would say, "Audrey Elaine, we did our best lunch ever Thursday!" My sister and I would grin. Another Morgen's record broken.

This is how they met: "I was sixteen, visiting my friend Edna in the building," Mom says. "And she read a letter she'd received from a boy who was going to the University of West Virginia. It wasn't a romantic letter, but it was such a no-nonsense and poetic letter, and I hadn't realized that boys could write interesting letters. I just felt they wrote about themselves playing football or jumping or something, and this was really an *interesting* letter. And I knew enough to know that this was somebody who could make life very, very important. So I said to Edna, 'Boy, I'd love to meet him.' And she said, 'His family has just moved into the building. He's away at school, but his sister, who is our age, is in the building, and you'll meet her,' and shortly thereafter I did. And I didn't know how to get an introduction to her brother, so I suggested to her that *my* brother would be in for spring vacation from Lafayette and I'd like him to meet her, and she said, 'Oh, I have a brother at the University of West Virginia, but he isn't coming in till June.' And I said 'Well, I'll have my brother call you when he comes in for spring break.' And my brother did and they dated when he was in town and she was available.

"In June of that year on the house phone, her brother called and he said, 'Are you free tonight? I'd like to take you out.' It was a Wednesday night June fifteenth, and he came down to the apartment, and my bedroom door could be a little ajar so I could peek at the front door. And our housekeeper, Alma, answered the door, and I saw this *wonderful*-looking young man standing there, and I was all atremble. I couldn't believe that this was going to be this blind date. He wasn't called Cecil then. His name was Stuff Volk. Everybody called him Stuff. His sister Helen was Big Stuff. His sister Harriet was Little Stuff. I called him Stuff until we married. I didn't think it was seemly to call a husband Stuff.

"That night, as I was buttoning my dress—it was a beige dress with a lotta lotta buttons down the front, and my hands were trembling so I couldn't button them—that night I said to myself, What are you so nervous about, Audrey? You'd think you were meeting your future husband. And then I came out, and we went on our first date, and he took me down to a pizza parlor in the Village. I had never had pizza. And he ordered one with anchovies on it, and I thought, Now I will surely die, because I had never eaten an anchovy and I had no intentions of doing so. But my next thought was, if I don't eat this, this very sophisticated young man who's in college is never going to take me out again. So I managed to bite and swallow without much chewing. And I think we took the Number 5 Fifth Avenue bus home, which stopped at Riverside Drive, so that we could walk to 845 West End Avenue, to our apartments. The next day I thought he wasn't very interested in me, because I hadn't heard from him by one o'clock in the afternoon. So I took out my two-wheeler, and I told the doorman to ring the new people's apartment and ask Harriet Volk to look out the window. But as I'd hoped, he came to the window, and he put his head out six stories up and said, 'Hi! What are you doing tonight?' while I was riding my bike. And I said, 'Nothing,' so we saw each other again that evening, and we saw each other every evening until June twenty-third, and that night we went to Glen Island Casino. We doubled with his sister and my brother, and I think Glenn Miller was playing there. We danced, and he gave me his class ring, and I was so thrilled, and that was the beginning."

Two years later, on June twenty-third, they got married. "He never had a chance of escaping," Mom says.

Now I'm getting married, and the only thing I've ever made is chocolate pudding.

"Mom," I say, "what'll I do? I don't know how to cook."

"There's nothing to it, darling." She gets up from the table and comes back with a cookbook written by a local woman who teaches cooking in adult ed: *The Menu-Cookbook for Entertaining* by Libby Hillman. "All you have to do is follow a recipe. Here. Just open the book. Any page."

I open the book. Mom takes it from my hands.

"Breast of Chicken in Madeira," she reads.

"I can't do this, Mom."

"See where it says ingredients? You buy them. See where it says six halves of chicken breasts, boned? You don't have to do that yourself. Ask the butcher. And then you just do everything the recipe says in that order."

For the next year, anytime anyone comes to dinner, they get Breast of Chicken in Madeira. I get pretty good at Breast of Chicken in Madeira. I get so good, when I take the cookbook out, it automatically opens to page 96. When I've mastered Breast of Chicken in Madeira, I invite my parents. I look through Libby Hillman for more recipes and pick out the things that sound the most delicious: Grilled Shrimp in Cream Sauce for an appetizer, and to go with the Breast of Chicken in Madeira, Tossed Salad with Creamy Cheese Dressing, Mushrooms in Port and Cream, Brussels Sprouts with Heavy Sweet Cream, Cauliflower Pie with Grated Cheese and Sour Cream, and for dessert, Chocolate Mousse.

I want the meal to be memorable. It is.

I speak a language with my mother I share with no one else. It is the language of clothes. It recognizes and respects the power of white piqué and navy to signal spring. It honors what a good coat can do for you in the world. It appreciates the whimsy of Moschino and the darts of Armani and the humor in a gray wool sweater with a "fur" collar made of gray wool loops like the one we recently saw in the Boca Loehmann's. The sweater is on display. It is the last one.

"Isn't it wonderful!" I say.

"Yes," Mom agrees.

The saleswoman takes it down. It's the wrong size. Here my mother and I part company. I buy it anyway.

Bengaline, organza, faille, peplum, toque, tattersall, Dupioni, moiré, paillette, ottoman, ruche, pavé, crepe de chine, plissé, revers, bouclé, blouson, bombazine. Lamé. Bolero, Eton, mandarin. I love to say these words aloud, words I use only with my mother. We describe clothes with exquisite economy: "It was a midnight-blue peau de soie djellabah with Alice blue passementerie and raglan sleeves," the language of clothes being every bit as exotic and operatic as the language of food: *Praline, persillade, caul. Carrageen, clafouti, capelli d'angelo. Bain-marie, friandise, rouille. Evasée, risotto, chinois. Sautier, demiglace, Parmigiano-Reggiano.*

Flipping through the racks at Loehmann's with my mother, I feel like a shark nosing out the kill. No, I feel like the shark's *baby* who learns by watching its mother. Mom is still the best-dressed woman in the room. She's still the prettiest girl there, wherever there is.

A unt Honey's twin grandsons are being bar mitz-vahed in California. I go with Mom for a fitting. She's bought a German-designed black evening suit. It's off the shoulders, but not décolleté, a twelve-inch cuff exposes her down to just above the start of her cleavage. It's cut straight over delicately flared pants. The effect is like a bust of my mother on top of a black column. (It helps to be a hipless size 6.) Mom likes the outfit, but she wants the top to taper slightly then flare. She thinks the pants will look better if the inseam has a touch less fabric.

I sit in a chair at the boutique while three people wait for my mother to emerge from the dressing room: The saleswoman, the dressmaker, and the owner of the store. Mom steps up on the platform in front of the three-sided mirror. I am plunged back into my youth, my mother studying herself critically in the mirror, pointing where she thinks the pins should go. She knows what she wants. That's something she radiates.

"A little here . . . a little here . . . Um-hmmm . . . No . . . Um-hmm. What about this?"

The store people hover. They fret. They move pins and look at my mother looking at herself as she dips and turns.

After half an hour I start wandering around the boutique. There isn't one thing I'd wear. The only thing I like from this store is what my mother has on. Did she find the one good thing? Or does it just look so gorgeous because she's wearing it?

There's a mini-conference going on about the length of the pants. Finally Mom's ready to go. The saleswoman, the dress-maker, and the owner of the store seem anxious but pleased. A job well done. Or so we think. The next day the phone rings. The owner needs Mom to come back. She thinks there may have been an error. Something with the pinning may not be 100 per-cent right. She needs another opinion. The best dressmaker they have is coming in today and she'd like her to check my mother before they actually cut fabric.

We go back. Mom gets repinned. Then we head for the Boca jewelry exchange. Mom needs a necklace to go with the outfit. Joel, her Florida jeweler, has just the thing—a gold and diamond sunburst. My mother's head is the sun, the sun's rays are gradu-ated diamonds beaming out of her neck. The necklace needs nothing. It is perfect.

Audrey Morgen Volk and her darling brother, Robert Irwin Morgen.
No flowers were allowed in the apartment while he was overseas.

MALLOMARS

Conventional wisdom is evanescent. It's true, but only as long as it's true. Conventional wisdom lasts as long as a haircut. It's truth for the time being. For three years my family lined up for fish-oil pills every morning because the Inuit, whose diet is largely fish, were reported to have the lowest rate of heart attacks. For three years we had fish-oil breath. Now it turns out it's low stress that makes Inuits live longer.

Tofu has fat in it.

Yogurt causes cataracts in rats.

If you wait long enough, anything that's bad for you gets good for you. And anything that's good for you gets bad. This got me angry until I learned people who scored high on the Hostility Scale were at greater risk for mortality than smokers. Then the Mayo Clinic announced there's no link between hostility and health. So when I think of Uncle Bob's childhood and the beatings he took from my grandfather, I have to remember that conventional wisdom from biblical times through the forties was, "Spare the rod, spoil the child." Today we have Dr. Fitzhugh—

"You can't spoil children, you can only spoil fruit"—Dodson. Today my grandfather would get hard time.

"A home wasn't run the way it is now," my mother says. "It wasn't a democracy. We had no voice unless we took an action."

"What do you mean?"

"Like when my father went to hit Bob when he was fourteen, and Bob grabbed his arm and said, 'If you do it, I'm going to hit you back,' and that was the end. My brother never got hit again. But he used to get beatings—terrible beatings—with a strap."

Aunt Barbara comes in from Arizona, and we meet at Bergdorf's for the Gotham salad. I call Aunt Barbara Tanta Barbara because she came from a religious family, and sometimes because she was so loyal to Uncle Bob, Tonto.

"Did you love Poppy?" I ask her.

"Your grandfather was a great man."

"Yes, but did you love him?"

"Yes."

"How could you? He was cruel to Uncle Bob."

"He was remarkable, your grandfather. He was a genius. He was your uncle Bob's father."

"That's why you loved him?"

"Your grandfather was a great man."

World War II is over. I am meeting Uncle Bob for the first time. I know three things about him.

1. Uncle Bob is my mother's brother.
2. My grandmother refuses to have flowers in her apartment. How can you enjoy beauty while your boy is overseas?
3. My grandfather has sold three restaurants and retired from the business because it is un-American to deal in black-market meat and there is no legal way for a restaurant man to get enough.

But now the war is over. My grandfather is opening a new store on West Thirty-eighth Street in the garment center, four blocks from Madison Square Garden and in the shadow of the old Metropolitan Opera. A built-in customer base for lunch and dinner. Uncle Bob and my father will join him.

I ask for the Mallomars. Mattie gives me a plate. The doorbell rings. My sister and I race to open it. Uncle Bob is slim and almost as tall as Dad. He wears a uniform and a matching hat with a polished visor. We stare up at him. He is stunningly handsome. We have ourselves a real-life hero.

"Would you like some Dentyne?" Uncle Bob says.

He gives us each a stick.

In the living room he sits on a green upholstered chair and lets us try his hat on. I take the Mallomar plate off the coffee table.

"Would you like a Mallomar?"

"Thank you, darling." He opens his mouth, puts a whole one on his tongue, and closes his mouth around it. His lips don't move as he chews. We eat Mallomars in licked layers. We have contests to see how long a Mallomar can last. I ask him the thing I want to know: "Did you ever see a dead person?"

"Yes," he says.

"What did he look like?"

Uncle Bob takes his time answering. "Like he was sleeping, darling."

"Was he bleeding?"

"Let's talk about something else."

"Would you like another Mallomar?"

L ove for Uncle Bob was steeped in sadness: my grandfather's abuse, getting sent off to Kyle Academy when he was nine, then the New York Military Academy when he was thirteen. He was happiest playing the clarinet, solo or accompanying Benny Goodman on a seventy-eight. Originally Uncle Bob studied saxophone. But when he shipped out to Pearl Harbor, my grandmother mailed him a clarinet because it was easier to tote around a war. He never went back to the sax.

At Thursday night dinners, sometimes Uncle Bob could be persuaded to take his clarinet out of my grandmother's hall closet and play. He'd snap the black leather case open and lift the four sections of his silver-keyed "licorice stick" from their fitted purple velvet compartments. He'd screw the mouth and the bell to the body parts. He'd study the reed and scrape it with a knife. He'd lick and suck it. Then he'd take a deep breath, go limp, and the sound would come. Sometimes it shrieked. Sometimes it crooned. When he played it low and throaty, it snarled. He played with his eyes closed, eyebrows clenching when the sound came out and unclenching when he gaped the mouthpiece for air. His cheeks ballooned. His knees folded, and his body swayed. The family sat quiet around the table while he swelled and contracted. Uncle Bob was transported. For ten minutes he's not thinking about the war, I would think. For ten minutes he's not thinking what a disappointment he is to his father.

There in our midst, in our family, was an artist. Watching him, I knew if I had any hope for happiness, I'd better find work I loved.

Between songs we'd rave. We'd fan our hearts.

"Aw, c'mon." Uncle Bob would look down.

"Encore! Encore!" We'd clap. " 'Moonlight Serenade'!"

"No." He'd start taking the clarinet apart. "That's it."

"My brother was gifted," Mom says. "He would have had a better life if he'd been a jazz musician."

In the store there was no music. Who would have heard it? There was too much laughter. Too much meeting and greeting. The night of the 1965 New York blackout, even with no electricity, it was a party, more so than usual. Why go home? Elevators weren't working, and who wants to climb twenty flights to sit alone in the dark? Dad put candles on the tables. The stove was gas, the food kept coming. The goal at Morgen's was beyond good food. Everyone should have a good time.

Behind the swinging doors was another story. My grandfather threw plates at his son. They raged. They cursed. China sailed above the sauté station and crashed against the prep table. Line cooks ducked. Dishwashers trembled. In the steaming, sizzling, manic, yellow-tiled airless kitchen, where every day was the stateroom scene from the Marx Brothers' *Night at the Opera,* they exploded. Uncle Bob managed the kitchen, but there was nothing he could do that pleased my grandfather. In his sixties he went to the doctor to get a fish bone removed from his throat. He needed an endoscopy. Like his father, Uncle Bob refused anesthesia. Then he winced. "I'm sorry." He apologized to the surgeon. "My father never would have done that."

"He would hit the wall to stop himself from hitting your grandfather," Aunt Barbara says. "I'd know they were fighting when I'd see the bookkeeper moving pictures off the wall."

It's occurred to me that my grandfather was so hard on his son because my grandmother loved Bob so much. She had prodigious love, more than enough to go around. She loved Yeatsian-style, "overmuch." But when Bob was born, my grandfather must have understood that no matter how much love my grandmother had, he would have to share what had once been all his. And for the rest of her life my grandmother would negotiate uneasy teary truces between the two of them. It could be that, or it could be my grandfather couldn't forgive Uncle Bob for not being like him. He couldn't respect his son's singularity. Maybe it's both.

I loved Uncle Bob the delicate way you love someone you think lives with tragedy. I asked him questions so he'd talk about himself. I kissed him up. Like his father, Uncle Bob didn't say good-bye when he hung up the phone. He said, "Love you, darling," *then* slammed it down.

Uncle Bob made it to corporal during the war but got busted back to private first class for refusing to wear shoes. When he came home, my grandparents introduced him to Barbara Krass, daughter of their card-playing cronies Faye and Lou. There's a picture of Aunt Barbara around this time in a scoop-necked blouse. A black velvet ribbon threads through eyelet at the neck and ties in a slender bow. The picture is airbrushed into an oval vignette, like a cameo. Wallets and frames came with movie stars' pictures like this at the five-and-ten. (Calling Woolworth's a five-and-*dime* was one of the countless ways people revealed their lack of gentility.) Aunt Barbara was a movie star. Heroic Uncle Bob and gorgeous Aunt Barbara, our very own family romance. As their wedding drew close, Mom had matching white organdy dresses made. We got new Mary Janes at Indian Walk. We were given our first white gloves. We were going to be flower girls at The Ritz-Carlton and carry lily-of-the-valley bouquets that matched the lily-of-the-valley embroidery on our dresses.

I luffed around in a romantic haze. Finally the big day came. My sister woke up flushed. She didn't feel well. Mom read the thermometer. She had 102.

"You have to stay home with your sister," Mom said.

"No, I don't."

"Yes, you do."

"But I was invited! I got an invitation!"

"If she can't go, you can't go."

"Yes, I can."

"You can't. And that's final."

I cried. I begged. I went back to the bedroom where my sister was reading the Classics Illustrated No. 42, *The Swiss Family Robinson*. I grabbed it out of her hands and sailed it out the window.

"I'm gonna kill you," she said, throwing off her covers.

"You're not allowed out of bed." I backed away. "I'm telling."

"You're dead," she said, grabbing a hairbrush.

"Go ahead. Kill me. I'll die happy knowing you'll spend the rest of your life in jail. Come on. Come on. I hope you fry."

She swung her feet back under the covers and turned on the radio. Later I made her chocolate pudding.

I'm in college when one day, out of the blue, my mother says, "I can't imagine why I didn't let you go to Uncle Bob's wedding."

Then, ten years after that, when I'm married with kids of my own, we're washing dishes together, and suddenly she says, "You know why I didn't let you go to Uncle Bob's wedding?"

"Why?"

"It must have been because you were sniffling. I must have been afraid you were coming down with something too. What other reason could there be?"

Ten years after that, when she's studying for her master's in family counseling, she tells me she knows exactly why she didn't let me go.

"You didn't want to go to Uncle Bob's wedding," she says. "You didn't feel comfortable going without your sister. You wanted to stay home with her."

"Is that how it was, Ma?"

"Don't you remember? You wanted to stay home. Otherwise I would have let you go."

"Oh," I say.

"You don't believe me?"

"It's been so long, Ma. Thirty years."

"Well, that was it," my mother says. "It has to be."

"It doesn't matter anymore," I say. "I never think about it."

"Well, that's what happened."

When Uncle Bob was inducted into the army, he was supposed to be in for six months or a year. Then the war came. He peeled "mountains of potatoes." He hated KP. The kitchen job he didn't mind was scrambling eggs. They used powdered eggs for the enlisted men, but Uncle Bob figured out how to make them seem real. "For every gallon of powdered eggs, I'd crack one real egg in, shell and all. If you have to pick a little piece of shell off your tongue, you think you're eating real eggs."

When the war was over, Uncle Bob was shipped from Saipan to California. Then his unit took a train to the discharge center in New Jersey. He called his parents and said he was on his way home.

"We'll be right there!" they said.

"No," Uncle Bob said. "Don't come. If I'm held up, I'll lose my place, and they'll put me back at the end of the line, and it'll take me another few days to get home."

"Okay," they said. "We won't come."

But that night my grandfather shot up in bed and said, "We're going."

The next day Bob was discharged. When he got to New York, his parents were in New Jersey. Uncle Bob went downtown to Robert's Bake Shop on Eighteenth and Sixth, a place he'd never seen. He went to find my father, who was saving half the profits from the store for Bob. Dad thought that was fair. Why should Bob be penalized for money he could have earned if he wasn't serving his country? Why should Dad keep it all when Uncle Bob got $18.75 a month from Uncle Sam?

In 1960 Uncle Bob fell off a ladder in the restaurant and fractured his skull. He was on the critical list for eight days. In the end, the only residual damage was to his olfactory nerve. He lost his sense of smell and his sense of taste. Always a lean man, Uncle Bob began to eat. He kept eating and eating, getting bigger and bigger. He was a restaurant man who couldn't taste. He spent the rest of his life trying. Salty things like pickles, sweet things like caramel, anything steeped in vinegar, extremes of sweet, salt, sour, bitter. They felt different in his mouth. They produced, if not a taste, a sensation.

"He never smelled or tasted anything again?" I ask my father.

"If you quickly opened a bottle of ammonia and held it under his nose, he could smell that."

Uncle Bob and Aunt Barbara spent years building their dream house in Scottsdale, Arizona. They'd unroll the floor plans as if they were opening a Christmas present. The house was ingenious. Aunt Barbara had a bad knee, so they built it knowing someday she'd have trouble. It had ramps instead of steps. Wall sockets were waist high. Pool access was graded.

By the time the Morgen's East lease was up, the Arizona house was ready. They packed up and sold their place in New Rochelle. Aunt Barbara had a garage sale. Of the things no one bought, she gave me a music box and a pair of long white doeskin gloves made by Elsa Schaparelli. The stitches were invisible, the leather light as Kleenex. But the gloves were so narrow they wouldn't fit my five-year-old. I donated them to the Metropolitan Museum of Art in the name of Mr. and Mrs. Robert Morgen. I tried to strike a deal with the curator in the Costume Institute. In exchange for the gloves, I wanted tickets for a sold-out lecture being given by Rosamond Bernier. The curator thanked me for the gloves but turned down my request. I couldn't bear missing that lecture. It was going to be about Miss Bernier's early days in Paris, meeting Picasso and starting *L'Oeil*. I wrote her a letter and told her the story. "How could I resist such a plea?" Miss Bernier wrote back. She mailed me two house seats for the going rate.

The Lieban girls—Gertie, Polly, and Ruthie—
in their black dresses and princess-length pearls

The phone rings. It's 6:30 a.m.

"Did I wake you?" my sister says.

I tell her the dream: "We went for a walk. A deer was lying on the sidewalk. Two dogs had eaten its innards and were licking their chops. The deer kept trying to stand up. It didn't know it was dead. Its baby, a black goat, watched from across the street."

"Wow!" my sister the therapist says. "That's the worst dream I ever heard."

I make a pot of coffee. My friend Brenda calls. "I need a jacket," she says. "My jacket's shot to hell."

"Mine too."

We meet after work and head up Madison. Two women pass us wearing The Jacket. The Jacket was designed for a purpose, so it defies trends. It's a seventeenth-century alpine boar-hunting jacket. It comes with options, like a car.

"Oh, look!" I point to a store window. "They have The Jacket!"

We go into the store. The Jacket is $695 stripped, without the lining, without the hood.

"Jackie had three of them in mushroom." The saleslady flips to one the color of dirt.

She holds up another jacket. It's the color of phlegm.

"Moss would match your eyes," she says.

"When does The Jacket go on sale?" I ask.

"Never," the salesperson huffs. "It only goes up."

At Fifty-ninth Street, standing in front of us, a woman is wearing The Jacket. Something about her looks familiar. It's Aunt Harriet.

"Hi, Aunt Harriet," I say.

She looks at me. "Who are you?" she says.

Aunt Harriet is Little Stuff, my father's younger sister. His older sister, Aunt Helen, never recognizes me either.

"It's Patty," I say. "Your niece."

"Patty! Well, for Pete's sake! How's your dad?"

We chat till the light changes. When Aunt Harriet is out of sight, Brenda cracks up. I have to explain that for reasons I've never understood, neither of my father's sisters ever recognizes me. I grew up with them, we had Thanksgivings together, I look just like my father, but when I run into his sisters, I have to tell them who I am.

We give up on the jacket and say good-bye. It's too late to start dinner. I pick up some Kentucky Fried Chicken. It costs $10.99 for a ten-piece bucket, even though the KFC commercial says it costs $8.99.

At dinner no one wants the chicken. I've reheated it in extremis so you can't taste how greasy it is. There are some foods that are better over-hot, that get inedible as their temperature drops. Gummy soup. All fast food. Fried scungilli. Fried anything except bacon, which is good no matter how cold it gets. Stew.

A pizza will take forty minutes. The kids are not happy. That's when I think of it: Aunt Gertie's meat loaf. Whenever I make Aunt Gertie's meat loaf, I make two. One for dinner, one for the freezer. It's a form of security. This is what microwaves are for.

At five feet ten inches, Aunt Gertie was the tallest of the three sisters. She was also the firstborn, so she got to accompany her father on trips. Louis Lieban was a hat drummer. He went up and down the East Coast with his daughter selling hats. All the sisters had what was called a hat face. They looked good in hats, knew how to put them on. You can give a beautiful hat to a beautiful woman, but if she doesn't know how to wear it—the right angle, the right attitude—it can look dopey or worse. Whereas a woman who might seem ordinary, in the right hat she becomes a siren, a vamp, a pixie, a coquette, a dependable human being, someone to be reckoned with, innocent or mysterious. A hat more than any other article of clothing creates an instant persona. A good hat has an idea. It's a frame for your face. Too bad women don't wear hats in America much anymore. They're a shorthand for telling people who you think you are in the world, who you want to be. The taking off and putting on of a hat is a small piece of theater. Even when there is no audience, the act of putting on a hat is performed, it gets you into character. Think of the simple Basque beret, the many ways to wear it, what each way means and how each way makes you feel. Think how color options modify that.

Aunt Gertie preferred sophisticated hats with drama. She had perfect posture, and no matter what life flung at her, walked as if she were being coronated. She wore my mother's old suits as if they'd been fitted by Balenciaga. She wore my grandmother's cast-off furs draped loosely like Maximillian's. My grandmother was shorter and bulkier than Gertie, but certain fur coats are sizeless: a sheared swing beaver, a single-breasted mink with revers, a Russian broadtail greatcoat with a shawl collar. Aunt Gertie didn't get anything first. Even her money was secondhand. When my grandmother began getting Social Security, she signed the check over every month.

A unt Gertie had one child, Wallace Shultz. During his birth, bacteria entered Aunt Gertie's bloodstream. Antibiotics weren't in use yet. She was dying of sepsis, and Wally, unnursed, was what the hospital called failing to thrive. Polly had given birth to my mother three months earlier, so on the pretext of visiting Gertie, she sneaked into the nursery and stole Wally. When she got home, she dialed the hospital. "Don't look for him," my grandmother said. "I got him."

Polly breast-fed Wally along with my mother, fattening him up while her sister rallied. (Gertie never got over not being able to nurse her son. She poured heavy sweet cream on Wally's cereal every morning of his life till the day he got married.) Wally grew into a dashing black-haired man, six feet three, tall like Gertie, with her delicate nose, leading-man handsome. But as an infant, there was a stunning anomaly. Wally was born with too much hair. It didn't stop at his forehead. It went down to his eyebrows. The sides of his face to below his ears were napped like an ape's. He was Wally the Wolfbaby.

My grandmother wasn't worried. Newborn hair usually falls out. His forehead would grow. She went to work. She stitched up a drawstring cap that, when tightened, covered Wally's brow and cheeks. Only his eyes, nose, and mouth showed. When Aunt Gertie was ready to leave the hospital, Nana wrapped Wally in a receiving blanket and pulled on the hat. Aunt Gertie had never seen her son. From the divan in Polly's bedroom, she stretched out her arms.

"Bring me my son," she said.

Nana carried the little bundle in. Aunt Gertie reached for him. She kissed him. "I can't see his face," she said. She untied the cap and pushed it back. She fainted.

L ike everyone in the family (except Granny Ethel), Aunt Gertie met her husband on a blind date. Dike Shultz was a tall courtly gentleman from Greensboro, North Carolina, whose manners were widely admired. His family owned a department store but threw him out when he misappropriated some money. Dike Shultz turned out to be a compulsive gambler. My grandfather set him up in Herman's Luncheonette at 284 Pearl Street near the courts, but Dike didn't have the disposition for restaurant work. He couldn't hurry.

"Nobody was fast like my father." Mom laughs. "He had wheels."

Dike reduced his family to poverty, moved to Washington, D.C., then died there of pneumonia. Dike Shultz, the gambler. I was certain, growing up, that he was really Dutch Schultz the racketeer, that he'd been upgraded to gambler for the sake of appearances.

Penniless, Aunt Gertie had to move out of apartment 2C in the family building, 845 West End Avenue. She moved around the corner to a small first-floor apartment on 101st Street and Riverside Drive. My grandfather offered her a restaurant to manage, but she wanted to be home for Wally. Then my grandmother got an idea. Gertie would take in "a line." From her apartment she would represent a dress manufacturer and show his clothes. My grandmother called her brother Jerry in Norfolk, where he had the children's department at Rice's Department Store.

"Gert needs a line," Polly told him. "See if you can get Gert a line."

Gert got a line. But how do you lure customers to 101st Street to try on dresses in an apartment?

"Get these sizes," my grandmother said, and handed her sister a slip of paper. On it Polly had written the sizes of all the women in the family. For a year the family only wore dresses from the line, but the customer base never increased. Aunt Gertie went under.

She had taste. She was refined. She got a job as a saleslady at Sachs Thirty-fourth and brought Wally up on her own.

"Gert, you're so good," the sisters would say. "Why don't you work at Saks?"

"I like Sachs," she'd answer. "I feel safe there. They know me."

Nineteen years after Dike died, Aunt Gertie had her first date. By this time she was forty-seven. The next morning, she called my grandmother to report.

"He had a car," she told Polly. "But a terrible overcoat."

"He has a car?" Polly said. "He can take you places, and Herman will buy him a new overcoat."

"He had hair in his ears."

"He can go to Herman's barber."

"His hankie wasn't pressed."

"Look," my grandmother said, "the rod in your guest closet is down. He could put it up, Gert."

"For a dollar I can have the superintendent put it up."

The few times people introduced Aunt Gertie to a man, she found something unforgivable. "He had bad breath, darling." She would wrinkle her nose. "There was dirt under his fingernails." In all, she had four dates. Her last date ever, I asked Aunt Gertie how she liked him.

"He used my *bathroom*." She shuddered.

"What happened? Did he leave the seat up?"

"You don't want to know, darling."

"Yes, I do."

"A *spatterer*." She rolled her eyes.

Once, I asked Aunt Gertie if she missed being held by a man. "I never liked the he-she thing," she said.

A unt Gertie played the piano by ear. She had a nice singing voice. "She could always be fun," according to my mother, "if the situation allowed it."

"What does that mean, Ma?"

"She could sit at the piano and play."

For family gatherings we'd drive downtown to the southern reaches of Stuyvesant Town, a postwar Howard Roark–pure complex that 25,000 New Yorkers in 8,755 apartments called home. Opened in 1947 for World War II veterans, it covered eighteen square blocks. Stuyvesant Town was another Robert Moses big dream, this one financed by Metropolitan Life. We'd pick Gertie up at her Fourteenth Street entrance and drive her to Mom's. I'd get in the back with my children, and she'd sit rigid in the front, directing all comments to the windshield. When my daughter had trouble hearing her, she'd scream, "Look around, Ger-treeeeeee!" Then we'd laugh and start eating her glossy butter cookies.

"Darling, make sure you return the tin," Aunt Gertie would say in her normal voice. On the phone she had another voice. Although Aunt Gertie never allowed pets, she spoke to me the way I spoke to mine. Aunt Gertie spoke cutesy-poo. She mimped. *Ooo dat?* for Who's that? *Owsh my pwecious widdle dirl?* *Yesh* for Yes. And her favorite: *In't see koot?*

At my grandmother's Thursday-night dinners, after my sister and I had performed a duet like "A You're Adorable, B You're So Beautiful," or put on the latest version of "Pat and Jo's Showboat," after the adults had been seated, it was customary to walk around the table and kiss each one hello. "Hello, Aunt Lil!" "Hello, Aunt Ruthie!" Some used their thumb and first finger to squeeze your cheeks together and say, "Could you eat her up?" Some patted. Aunt Gertie pinched. Fast as a lizard, she'd swing her right hand out of her lap and drive it up my dress, then under my underpants. She pinched my naked behind as if she were working hard clay. It never occurred to me to protest. I assumed I was supposed to like it. Aunt Gertie loved me. Why would she do it if it wasn't right? I put pinching in the category of Things Done to Me I Don't Like That Must Be Okay: Dr. Bronstein, the dentist, who rubbed my right breast with his forearm when he drilled, Cosmé McMoon, the piano teacher who slapped my hands, Miss Haas, the teacher from P.S. 9 who called me Volk instead of Patty. "Volk, get over here!" There comes a time when you know some things are wrong. Until then it's open season on children. Dr. Smith, the allergist, who asked my mother to leave the room, then gave me a vaginal exam when I was eight. It's like the Jean Rhys story, the one about the old sea captain who visits the windward islands and takes the pretty young girl for walks, and one day, as they're chatting, he shoves his hand down her blouse and lays it on her breast, and she thinks, Surely, it was a mistake.

Widowed, broke, alone, Aunt Gertie raised Wally then followed him to Florida when he went to the University of Miami. She wanted to make sure he took his cereal with cream. When Wally married a local girl who didn't like her, Gert moved back to New York to be with people who did. Wally and his wife became hairdressers, and when he came north to visit, he would do Gertie's hair. It was white by that time, and he styled it beautifully, massing it up, making more of it.

Aunt Gertie had her appendix removed, her ovaries, her uterus, her large intestine, parts of her small or vice versa. She had as many ectomies as you can have and still live. When she had pain, some things were automatically ruled out because they weren't there anymore. It can't be a gallbladder attack if you don't have a gallbladder. Eventually, something misfired in all seven of her vital organs, and she blamed whatever else happened on her diverticulitis.

I wish I had something that belonged to Aunt Gertie. When I got married, she gave me an electric blanket. But I was a newlywed, my husband was heat enough. I returned the blanket for some towels. I do have a photo of her, tall and timeless in a black taffeta dress with black lace over an illusion insert, a dress I would be happy to wear now. She's standing next to my grandmother Polly, who is standing next to Aunt Ruthie. The Lieban girls are smiling in their princess-length pearls. So I have that wonderful picture of the three sisters, and I have Aunt Gertie's recipe for meat loaf. She told me her secret ingredient. It was ice water. She added half a cup per pound of beef. "It keeps the meat moist, darling," she said, and it does.

A unt Gertie shared her meat loaf secret, but she refused to share her friends. Polly would invite Gertie uptown to join her canasta game, but Gertie never invited Polly down to hers. It pained my grandmother. It puzzled her.

She was so good to Gertie. My mother postulated that Gertie fabricated her game, that she didn't really have one. She just wanted people to think she did. It's what William James said, If you act a certain way long enough, it becomes you. Aunt Gertie acted the role of the popular woman with a regular game, a woman in demand. Maybe she did have a game and just wanted to keep it to herself. It was the one thing she didn't depend on my grandmother for. Gertie used Nana's old lamps, her old sideboard, her old rugs and linens, cast-off everything but shoes. (Gertie's left was an eight, her right a nine, forcing her to always buy two pairs. In her sixties a doctor told her she'd once had a mild case of polio.) My grandmother was the sister with children right close by, the decorated apartment, clanking jewelry, the successful husband. Aunt Gertie depended on her largesse. People don't always like people they need. Centers of families are resented for being essential by the people who make them essential. The only power Aunt Gertie had in my grandmother's life was denying her the privilege of joining her weekly canasta game, if the game existed. And yet I could picture Aunt Gertie sitting in her tiny apartment, back ramrod-straight, staring out the window and not answering the phone on "game" days. She just said she had a game so everyone would think she had a life. It wouldn't surprise me. Aunt Gertie believed how she thought she appeared to people was how she was.

S o I take Aunt Gertie's meat loaf out of the freezer. "We're going to have Aunt Gertie's meat loaf!" I tell my children and pop it in the microwave. It comes out steaming, but the hard-boiled eggs are so hard I can't slice through them.

"Gross," my daughter says.

"Can we order Chinese?" My son looks hopeful.

We have raisin bran.

Hank Morgen tried to escape the Nazis on skis.
Here he teaches my son, Peter, to use them.

CUCUMBER SALAD

I met Uncle Hank at one of my grandmother's seders. By then he was in his fifties. My grand- mother's seders were the same as her Thursday- night dinners with the addition of the three M's: matzo, macaroons, and Manischewitz. And everybody got a hard-boiled egg. An egg has no beginning and no end. It symbol- izes eternal life. You dip the egg in a finger bowl filled with warm salt water, tears of mourning shed by Jews. You dip life into tears, then eat it. We set a place for the prophet Elijah and left the back door open. Elijah was the Jewish Santa, dropping by every house on the big night. We didn't have a Passover ser- vice. We didn't have prayer books. Our religion was getting to- gether at my grandmother's to eat. Once, on the swings in the playground, a little girl said to my sister, "I'm Catholic. What are you?"

"I'm Jo Ann," my sister said.

Hank showed up at the seder with his wife, Hedy. He nodded in an Old World way when we were introduced. He looked more like my grandfather than my grandfather's son did. Their eyes were the same gray. Their cheeks were flat planes. Both had a pinkie that didn't bend.

"How olt za children ah?" Hank beamed at them.

"How olt *ah* za children," Hedy corrected him.

"How olt *ah* za children?"

"Six and three," I said.

"Zay ski, ya?"

"They're too young!"

"No! Zay are ready. Peter! Polly! Ve go to ski together? I teaches zem, ja?"

"I *teach* zem." Hedy rolled her eyes.

Hank lit up when he saw us. We lit back. What good luck to discover new and loving family. A ski trip was planned. Suddenly the four of us were spending New Year's with Hank and Hedy at a ski lodge, sipping champagne and downing port-soaked prunes broiled in bacon.

They came for dinner. They visited us on vacation. They joined us for the holidays. Gifts arrived. Hank ran an office-supply company. I'd come home from work, and there outside my door would be a lifetime supply of black plastic garbage bags. A box of Quick Dry Wite-Out. A state-of-the-art stapler or a half gallon of rubber cement. A stepped set of Magic Markers and a gross of Pentels. A three-hole punch. In the hallway off our kitchen I labeled a cardboard carton UNCLE HANK'S BOX and filled it with binders, colored paper, glue sticks. Whenever the kids needed something for school, I'd say, "Check 'Uncle Hank's Box.' "

Hank reconnected to our family when he ran into my grandfather at a funeral. On Saturday afternoons, in the upstairs office at Morgen's East, they would drink schnapps and eat sturgeon. There was a frenzy of reckless speculation: What does Hank want? What's in it for him? Why the sudden interest? Aside from the Brooklyn Navy Yard restaurant swindle, no one had ever taken advantage of my grandfather except a young manager. Poppy loved Keith, "a German boy." Checks in the store were numbered in sequence. My father noticed some were missing. The con was simple. When people paid cash, Keith pocketed the money and tore up the chit. My grandfather refused to believe a German boy would do this. He went into mourning the day they let Keith go.

On ski trips I'd go antiquing with Hedy. I'd drive around all day and look for a hanging-fern place for lunch while she complained about Hank. I hated those weepy, whiny betrayals. Why speak ill of your husband to me? Why berate someone I adored? On one of our aimless rides Hedy told me she had gotten pregnant once but lost the baby when she stuck her hand in the blades of an electric fan. Hank and Hedy were it now, the only survivors of their families, survivors with no survivors, the ends of two lines.

The one time Hedy invited me to their apartment, she signaled I should follow her into her bedroom.

"Sit"—she pointed to the bed—"I have something important to tell you."

A great life lesson? I wondered. More complaints about Hank? But "Patty," she said, "when you have za money to buy jewelry, listen to me. *Never* buy three things by za same designer. Za most you can buy is two. You can buy a bracelet and earrings. You can buy earrings and a necklace. You can buy za necklace and za bracelet. But listen to me, never earrings, a necklace, *and* a bracelet. Two is elegant, Patty. Three is tasteless."

The first time I fixed cucumber salad for Uncle Hank he rested his wrists against the edge of the table. "Dahlink," he said, "vot you call zis?"

"Vot *do* you call zis!" Hedy pounced.

More than anything else I made, he loved that salad.

"Oooouf!" He'd grunt a punched-in-the-stomach sound. "Dahlink! Zis is *fobulous*!"

So whenever they came to dinner or lunch or joined us on a

picnic, I made cucumber salad with a variation of my grand-mother's salad dressing—a mayonnaise-based sauce with red wine vinegar, sugar, salt and pepper, and enough sour cream to make it thick enough for a fork to stand in it. I'd skin and seed the cukes, then slice them so thin they were transparent. I'd mix the sauce with a bunch of snipped dill and chopped parsley. I'd fold it all together and scrape it into a clear glass bowl so you could see the different greens.

"Dahlink, zis taste like heffen!" He would close his eyes.

"*Tastes* like heffen," Hedy would tsk.

When Hank skied, he'd tuck an Anjou pear in the chest pocket of his jacket. Survivors commonly secret food. Food and diamonds, and one man I know, every morning a knife in his sock. When Hank would come into the lodge for lunch, he'd unzip his jacket, dive his hand in, and, voilà!, produce the pear like a magician. He'd smile at the pear, hold it up between his thumb and first finger, squint. Then he'd put the pear on his tray, composing *Still Life with Pear and Styrofoam Cup of Chili*. Hank was an orderly man. He cared how things looked. He liked to dress. He had an eye.

Hank was the only survivor our family had. I wanted to know about his mother, Anna, and what her porcelain store was like in Nowy Targ and the Morgenbesser Tavern his father, Leopold, owned, and how Anna found out the Nazis were coming.

"She told me and my brothers to go to Russia," Hank said. "We would be safe there."

It was winter. The four brothers set out on skis. The next morning, when they opened their eyes, they were looking into the barrels of German rifles. The brothers were loaded onto a cattle car. They didn't have to wonder where they were going. Anna had told them what would happen if they got caught by the Germans. At night, when the train slowed, the brothers broke out.

"We were mountain boys. Dahlink, we run all day up za mountain. Is nothing. But the Nazis, *they have guns.*"

The Germans stopped the train. They flooded the mountain with searchlights and sprayed it with bullets. Hank kept running. When he was out of range, the Nazis sent dogs. Finally the Nazis turned off their lights. Only Hank and his brother Mundek were still running.

They recognized where they were. They headed home. In the morning Anna stuffed her remaining sons' clothes with sausage and cheese.

"Go to Russia!" She pushed them out. "Find the Russians and don't come back! The Russians are Allies! You'll be safe with them!"

This time Hank was more cautious. He and Mundek knew the mountain. They'd grown up skiing to school and every weekend in Zakopane. On the third day they crossed paths with the Russians. But instead of being welcomed, they were stripped of their coats and boots. Hank and Mundek marched barefoot to a work camp in Siberia. When I look at pictures in the paper of Chechen detainees in a Chernokozovo "filtration camp," I see the fear and misery on their faces. But I also see their high boots and down-filled jackets, and I wonder, How did he do it? How did Hank live?

When the Russian involvement in World War II intensified, Stalin decided he couldn't waste manpower monitoring prisoners. Hank and Mundek were released to the British. The British sent them by boat to Palestine and then on to Scapa Flow, in the north of Scotland. There, supervised by General Bill Anders, they became part of "Anders' Army" and joined a navy convoy.

"They give me one pair black socks," Hank said. "One. I *love* those socks. Every night, in the sink, I wash them out."

Hank trained as a medic, Mundek as a mechanic. When it came time to ship out, the brothers were put on different boats.

While Hank was at sea, an American air corps captain was shot down. Hank dove into the water and rescued him.

Hank was assigned to care for the airman's wounds. After the airman was sent home, a letter typed on stationery with a gold-embossed eagle arrived. "I don't read English, dahlink," Hank told me. "I have no idea what the letter say, but I think, Zis letter with za eagle, zis is important."

When Hank's ship docked in Glasgow, news arrived. Mundek had been killed. It was Yom Kippur.

"I went to *shul* to say *yiskah* for Mundek," Hank said. "Then, during the service, I hear my name. I turn around. There is Mundek who has come to say *yiskah* for me!"

By the time the war was over, Mundek was dead. He'd been shot down in his parachute. Hank also learned the rest of his family had been killed. No one was left. Only two relatives in America he'd never met. He didn't want to go back to Nowy Targ. Seven Jewish boys returned after amnesty looking for their families and were gunned down in cold blood. The war was over, but they were murdered by their neighbors.

Every day Hank lined up at the American embassy. Every day he was told the quota had been reached. Then he brought the letter with the eagle on it. The clerk read the letter. It was from the Secretary of Defense. It thanked Hank for saving the life of an American.

Hank was given a visa. He came to New York. Since L comes before M, he looked up the Lustigs instead of the Morgens. He went to live with Herman Lustig, his uncle in the restaurant business, instead of Herman Morgen, his other uncle in the restaurant business. Herman Lustig or Herman Morgen. You had to choose one. The Hermans didn't talk. Somebody had given playing cards as a gift that said "Compliments of American Air-lines." Or one of the wives got a mink coat, and when the other wife saw it she said, "Is that nutria?" Someone left a wedding too early or stayed too late or pretended not to see somebody passing them on Broadway.

So we didn't meet Hank until thirty-one years after he'd set foot on American soil. By then his hair was gray and because of this, although he was a cousin, we called him Uncle.

"I make za wrong choice," Hank would tell my grandmother. "I should hof come to you."

I was at the office the day Hank went in for explora-tory surgery. The phone rang around eleven.

"Patty! He has cancer," Hedy screamed. "All through his liver!"

A woman took the phone. "Are you a relative?" The voice was brisk.

"Yes."

"You need to come to the Hospitality Room right away."

When I got to the Hospitality Room, Hedy wasn't there. I found her in the Emergency Room. She was gulping for air like a fish on a dock, her first panic attack. The doctor said she had pal-pitations. "How I can live wizout him?" she wailed.

In between chemotherapy treatments, those hope-logged rallies when his taste buds came back and the nausea disappeared and his energy resurged, Hank would ski. He was grateful for every reprieve. He'd come to our apart-ment for dinner, and I'd make cuke salad for him, and radiant, a human source of light, he'd scoop up my children and shower them with Pilot extrafine rolling-ball pens.

"Dahlink"—he took me aside on one of these occasions—"you know what I don't understand? Why, out of everyone in my family, I was spared. Why should I be spared? For God to give me cancer? Can you tell me that, dahlink? Why *me?*"

The way he asked, it wasn't hypothetical. Hank really thought perhaps I could help explain it. I couldn't. How many people earn their fate? Suffering has never made sense. How should a survivor die? Quietly, at 104 in a soft feather bed? Or like my friend's grandmother? Mrs. Johnson dropped dead in her kitchen reaching for a box of cornflakes.

"Patty, dahlink," Hank said a week before he died, "you will take care of Hedy when I'm gone?"

"Yes."

"You won't forget her?"

"I promise."

Again the call at the office.

"Come!" she shrieks. I rush uptown. Hank is dead. In his room Hedy sits crying by the bed. He's still in it, the sheet pulled over his head.

"Look at him," Hedy says, ripping it down.

Hank is the color of a field mouse. His eyes are closed, but his mouth is in rictus. I want to touch him, but my hands won't move. Silently I say, I love you. I'm sorry. I know you don't want me to see you this way. I'll forget I saw you this way. I'll try. I love you. I will miss you, my darling dear. Thank you for being part of our lives.

Hedy comes to us for the holidays. We meet for lunch now and then. Soon she is saying how much she hates New York. Then she is saying that even though she hates New York, where else can she live? Florida is too hot. Canada, where she has a friend, is too cold. She doesn't know anybody anyplace else. Why is she always trapped? Finally she sells her apartment for less than she hoped and moves to Tamarack, Florida. As soon as she gets there, she hates it. It isn't near the beach. She doesn't drive. She sells the house at a loss and flies to Toronto, where the winters are too cold but the American dollar goes far. She finds a "friend," but he lives with his forty-eight-year-old son who is "a horse's you-know-what." Everything is a doomed proposition, like garlic-flavored mouthwash. Everything is unsolvable.

Afriend of mine is invited to a seder at a psychiatrist's house. At the end of the seder the host hands each guest a gift. It's a sheaf of paper, a photocopy of Schindler's List, the actual document. My friend offers me her copy. It's shocking to hold Schindler's List. It feels wrong to have it. A document lives hung on gets passed out like a party favor. Still that doesn't stop me from looking for the name Morgenbesser. There are two. Hedy is the last one alive who might know if these Morgenbessers were family.

I call her in Toronto. She calls a friend of Hank's. The Morgenbessers on Schindler's List don't match our family's given names. The names Hedy finds out, names I've never heard before, are the names of Hank's brothers who were murdered in the snow and his sister who was exterminated.

> Josef Morgenbesser
> Brunek Morgenbesser
> Nella Morgenbesser

The enduring image of someone you've loved is not necessarily your choice. It took fourteen years, but now when I think of Hank, I don't see his face in a hospital bed. I see him coming down a mountain. It was easy to spot him. Not because of his bright red ski suit with the white armbands or his yellow jumpsuit with the matching yellow boots. What set Hank apart was the way he skied. The top half of his body stayed still. His hips barely shifted. He looked as if he were dancing down the mountain—a sophisticated dancer, the kind who feels the music and conveys that using only the most economical gestures. Hank skied a way nobody else did. Even on a packed slope, you could pick him out. And that's how I can see him now, skiing and smiling, skiing to take your breath away. Hank made it look easy. I think he was a natural.

My gorgeous big sister

I've flown to Florida to take care of my best friend, the person who sees herself as always taking care of me, my big sister. I dial up from the hotel lobby.

"Don't be scared," she says.

"I can't wait to see you."

"Room three seventeen." She hangs up the phone.

I ride the elevator carbonated with expectation. What? *What?* The other two face-lifts I've seen had some mileage on them. My sister's face-lift is in its second day.

I knock. "Let me in, whee-oop!"

The door opens a crack. A hand snakes around. I know those fingers! I recognize those freckles! I know those squared red nails!

The door inches.

"Just open it," I say.

She does.

If someone fell from the top of the Empire State Building and landed on their nose, it couldn't be worse. I search the face for something that says I definitely have the right room. Luckily, my sister is wearing her old Victoria's Secret pajamas.

"I'm so glad you're here." She weeps.

"Wow!" I say.

"I *had* to do it." Tears flow from what used to be her eyes. "I haven't been able to look at my face while I brush my teeth for a *year.* Come." She shuffles toward the bed. With enormous effort my sister feels backward for the edge, sits, then swings her legs over until she can lean against the pillows. She does this like a Balinese dancer, without changing the flex of her chin. "Put your fingers on what's been done and tell me *everything.*" She lies there waiting. "I can't *seeeeeeee.*"

I examine what used to be my gorgeous big sister. I put a fingertip on the ventral side of her chin and run it side to side, an inch and a half. It's prickly. "There are stitches here," I say.

I look her over, then pat along her upper eyelids. Her eyes, her big brown eyes that danced when she smiled, are slits tilted at forty-five degrees. They are sewn partially shut. The micro-opening looks like a split seam. It is completely filled by brown eyeball, like something that lives underground. I trace the corners of her eyes where the thorny black stitches stick out. Then I finger her ears all the way around. The stitches make it look as if they've been cut off then sewn back on. There are hundreds of these tiny threads inside her ears too. They look like the almost invisible black trico flies I use to catch trout.

In her head, like croquet wickets, are rows of metal staples.

"These are staples." I drum my fingers all over her scalp. "And these are stitches."

"What about the screws?" she says.

I find those too.

"What about my *neck*?"

"It looks gajus," I say. "You're down to one chin."

"No. I mean *this.*"

We explore where the drain enters behind her ear. It's threaded down and inside, embossing her neck. The drain looks like a subcutaneous choker. A bloody liquid drips from the exposed part into a clear plastic bulb. Her upper lip, which has been derm-abraded to remove tiny vertical lines that used to wick lipstick, is oozing a thick yellow mustache. Because of the derm-abrasion, her lip is so swollen her words come out muffled.

"I think he did a really good job," I say. "The stitches are so neat."

I put fresh ice cubes and water in the small bowl beside her bed. She tells me how to ice her, two folded gauze pads on her eyes and cheeks and one unfolded flat across her forehead. Ice rolled in a towel on her neck.

"There's stuff on your tray," I say.

"You eat it."

The frittata is cold, so is the toast.

"Sure you don't want some?"

"Can't *chew*." She starts to cry again. "I don't know why I'm so *weepy*," she says. "It must be the *anesthesia*. It took *eight hours*."

My sister looks terrifying, and I don't know what to do. She reaches for the envelope with the pictures she'd shown the doctor.

"I want to look like this," she'd told him, fanning out photos from 1971.

"You will," he'd promised.

I want to be in water," my sister says through tears. I run her a warm tub. "Put some of that bath stuff in." She points to one of those little hotel bathroom freebies. "It's nice. I used it this morning."

"You used this in your tub?" I ask.

"Uh-huh," she says.

"It's hair conditioner."

"I couldn't *see*." She cries all over again.

I give her a bath, trying not to wet her hair, which sticks out in crazy greasy clumps. I rub her back with a soapy washcloth.

"That's soooo good," she moans. Afterward I rub her feet and the lower part of her legs with hotel body lotion.

"See," she says, "you *are* capable of empathy."

The doctor employs a nurse to watch his patients at the hotel. She comes in now and tells my sister there's a car downstairs to take her to the doctor's office. Still wobbly, my sister readies herself for the ride. In other words, she slips her mules on.

"Don't worry if anyone sees you in the lobby in your pj's," I say. "Really. There's no way they'd know it was you."

We close the hotel-room door behind us. The nurse is waiting. She is standing behind a wheelchair. The patient in it looks worse than my sister. This woman looks as if she fell off the Empire State Building, landed on her nose, then got run over by a Hummer. This woman had everything done my sister had done, plus wall-to-wall derm-abrasion. This woman is, quite literally, an open wound.

When we get to the doctor's office, I blurt: "Why is my sister so asymmetrical?"

"Where?" He takes it personally.

"Her eyes, her jawline." I'm not happy saying this in front of my sister, but maybe he can still do something. Am I supposed to praise a face that looks like a cake baked in an unreliable oven?

The doctor spins on his heel and storms out of the examining room. In a moment he is back, carrying a Pendaflex. He takes out the "Before" pictures he took of my sister. "Your sister was always asymmetrical," he points.

"I know most faces are," I say, looking at my sister's perfectly symmetrical Befores. Maybe we can't see asymmetry in faces we grew up with, faces we love. It occurs to me then that the reason symmetry is so pleasing is, it's the first thing we see. The first thing we see is our mother's face smiling down at us. Before we even know what seeing is, we know what feeds us and holds us is the same on both sides. On one side there's an eye. On the other there's an eye. There are two holes in the nose. And the mouth tilts up on both ends. When babies nurse, when they look at your face, you see their eyes darting, checking this out. Back and forth, back and forth, the symmetry, everything equal. It's reassuring hence peaceful. It's balanced. It's what we know.

I take my sister home and stay three days. I ice her, drive her to the doctor's, rent movies she can only hear because she still can't open her eyes. I monitor guests, field calls, talk to her patients, wash her, rub her, and bring her water. I save her from herself when she flaps her arms, throws a fit, and screams she's going to wash her hair no matter what.

"I'm going to wash my hair! I don't care! I don't care!"

"Please." I hold her arms down. "You've been through so much. You can't blow everything for a shampoo."

On the second day I ask her, since she can't chew, if she wants eggs for lunch.

"Yef," she says. Her speech is muffled because she still can't move her upper lip. "Make them Mattie's way."

"What's Mattie's way?"

On her back, her eyes and forehead covered with gauze, blood dripping into the drain, lips too traumatized to move right, my sister gives instructions.

"Let the butter melt on low. Very low. Don't let it brown or bubble, just melt. Use my small pan with the high straight sides. When the last bit of butter melts, drop four eggs in. Don't let the yolks break until the whites start to turn opaque. When the whites start to turn, run a fork through the eggs, breaking the yolks. Do that slowly." My sister uses one finger to make back-and-forth loops like the wire on a potato masher. It is a delicate gesture, something you'd expect to see in *Swan Lake*.

"You don't put any milk in?"

"Milk toughens eggs."

"No water?"

"No. Nothing. Just butter and eggs. Don't you remember the way Mattie made them? You could see little pieces of white."

"Yeah. I do. And the eggs were wet."

"Wet is very important."

I re-ice my sister, then go into the kitchen to make the eggs. I think of this face I have loved, the face I grew up with. My sister, the dark-eyed, raven-haired beauty. My beautiful big sister, the one who asked Mademoiselle Dryer, our French teacher, if they French-kissed in France. The great compliment of my childhood was, "Does anybody tell you you look like your sister?"

Maximum swelling comes seventy-two hours after surgery. Tomorrow my sister will look worse. Then she'll start to look better. But what does better mean? I loved her face before. I don't want it to look different. If she changes her outside, will her inside change too? I love my sister the way she is. Change is loss. I don't want to lose anything else in my life, especially my sister's face.

In the morning I brush my teeth in her guest bathroom and look at myself in the mirror. I'm getting Howdy Doody laugh lines. I don't have any wrinkles yet, but gravity's no pal. I'm ready to join the army of men and women who pose for photographs with their fists under their chins to take up the slack. Am I going to do it? I live in a culture where women start talking about plastic surgery in their thirties. Plastic surgery is like going to the dentist. What is my relationship to my face? I like my face. It's accessible. It's me people stop and ask, "Which way to Broadway?" or "What floor is lingerie?" People know from my face I won't hurt them. Occasionally someone says with surprise, "You know, you're actually kind of beautiful . . . in a way," as if he's discovered the tenth planet. What if the surgeon is having a bad day, and he severs a facial nerve, and I spend the rest of my life looking like a stroke victim? I like my face. We're friends. My face is my partner in crime.

Before I leave Florida, my sister takes eight additional tubs, turns green, opens her eyes a little more, tries to chew chicken curry (the doctor says she'll heal faster if she has protein), talks about our childhoods and our vastly different interpretations of identical experiences, makes note of who sent flowers, who sent books, who sent food, and who sent nothing, mentions that I really didn't rub her feet that much, cries a lot, and repeats herself. (It's the anesthesia.) She doesn't say a word about the eggs. I did everything she said to do, but I must have cooked them too long. They were so dry they had no shine. Five seconds is all it takes to overcook eggs scrambled Mattie's way. They're that delicate. And I couldn't salt them, because the doctor said salt prolongs the swelling. The eggs I made were a stranger's eggs. They didn't taste anything like Mattie's. If I had to pick something the eggs were like it would be rubber foam.

Dad

B O O S T

"Take a deep breath, Audrey!" Dad tells Mom. We're cruising up Palm Beach Lakes Road. Where Sapodilla Avenue meets the draw-bridge, there's an incline. You go uphill a little. "The highest elevation in Florida," Dad calls it.

"Fill those lungs, Audrey! We're going to the mountains!"

We pull into the driveway of Good Samaritan Hospital. In June, Dad gets his hip replaced, and his surgeon tells him, "Massive radiation is the new gold standard to prevent scarring." In July, Dad is diagnosed with myelogenous leukemia. In February it turns acute. Sixty percent of Dad's blood cells are in "blast." They've stopped working. As we wait for his first experimental chemo to kick in, Dad is kept alive by transfusions three times a week.

I come down twice a month. I know the drill. Dad gets an appointment. Regardless of the appointment, he gets to the office before it opens. Dad can't wait. He's wait-intolerant. The staff treats him with affection. Even strangers try to make my father happy. If his appointment is at noon, they take him at eight.

My sister and I give blood to see which one of us is the closest match for bone marrow. We never learn the results. Dr. Harris decides a bone-marrow transplant will kill Dad.

He gets on the scale. Before leukemia Dad weighed 242 pounds. Now he's 181. Not bad for a big-boned athletic man six feet one and a half. But Dad looks beaky. Mom checks the scale and sucks her breath in. Her line in the sand is drawn at 180, and Dad is now one pound from panic, one pound from being okay to not okay. It's like that nanosecond in the Holland Tunnel when half your body is in New Jersey, half in New York.

Julie, the tech, tries to find a vein. Dad's arm is a landscape of magenta hematomas. It's not her fault. His veins are minuscule. He's a big man with the veins of a fetus. Specialists are brought in. After rigorous slapping and hot compresses, they strike oil. Then it's an hour at least to find a blood-donor match and, when the match is found, another hour or two for the fluids and chemo to snake their way in. On a good day it's a five-hour deal with all the peanut butter crackers you can eat.

"I can't wait for this new chemo to kick in," Dad says about an experimental protocol out of M.D. Anderson: Ara-C swirled with Topotecan.

"I can't wait for this new chemo to kick in," Dad says about an experimental protocol from Dana Farber called Mylotarg.

"I can't wait for this new chemo to kick in," Dad says about Navelbine.

Dad wants to live. He computes how many minutes he has left on earth if he's lucky. It's a big number. One year alone is 525,600 minutes. He cautions all of his beloved children and grandchildren not to waste a one.

Because his father died when he was nine, Dad was sure he'd die young too. And because he was sure he would die young, I grew up believing I'd only have him a short time. Every next birthday we met with gratitude. He was living when he thought he was dying and dying when he was sure he would live.

We sit in the examining room. My father listens to the doctor, eager. "Now, Cecil," Dr. Harris says, "I want you to eat. Have breakfast three times a day if that's the food you can get down. You need twelve hundred calories a day at least. Drink Boost. You can't get better if you don't eat."

Dad loathes Boost, an artificially flavored dietary supplement. But an eight-ounce can of Boost Plus has 360 calories. He and my mother negotiate every sip.

"Just three more!" Mom says.

"Audrey, I can't."

"Just two. Just two and you're done!"

"I hate this crap."

"If you drain the glass, Cecil, I won't bother you the rest of the day. That's a promise."

Every long drag is her victory. Every turning away, her defeat. I make a DAD'S DAILY CALORIC INTAKE chart on his computer. I print out thirty and attach them to a clipboard. At night we total the calories.

"An egg is seventy-five."

"Yes, but I put butter on it."

"Is pudding the same as tapioca? What if you made the pudding with heavy cream?"

Dr. Harris is firm about the eating. Dad hangs his head. He can't chew. He can barely swallow what slides down. The chemo has done something vicious to the inside of his mouth. The nerves of his teeth are exposed. Eating and drinking are agony. One day, lying next to him in bed, I watch Dad's lips slip off. They turn white, quiver, and slough in clumps like wet Kleenex. Raw flesh is underneath.

At some point during this visit I tell Dad what I want to make sure I tell him: "I love you Dad. I love you without reservation. You have been the best father in the world to me. Thank you. Thank you for teaching me *Falco peregrinus* is the fastest animal on earth. Thank you for showing me everything has magic. Thank you for giving me your spurs from Colorado. Thank you for your sprawling embrace of the world. Thank you for showing me it's okay to break the rules. Thank you for everything you've taught me. I am widely envied for having you as my father. Always have been. *I* envy me. There is not a day that goes by I'm not grateful. I love you, love you, love you." I cover his face with kisses. "I love you so very much, Dad." By now I'm crying.

"Uh-oh," he says. "Here comes Niagara Falls. Here comes the waterworks."

"I (sob, sob) love (boohoo) ya, Daddy (waaaaaaaaa)."

"Cut the crap," he says.

We are on the cancer roller-coaster, the *cancer* coaster, the yea-boo yea-boo ride of a lifetime. Dad is bald now. Six months ago, before the hip surgery, he was playing tennis every day, tooling around Boca in his black leather jacket on his 1973 mint-condition BMW 750 CSR. Now he's tooling around in a wheelchair. He sleeps in the downstairs guest bedroom, and around five every morning I hear the determined tap-tap-*kuh*lap of the walker as he makes his way into his real bedroom to lie next to my mother. It's a long, hard journey between bedrooms. When I walk in at eight, there they are— Mom asleep on her back, Dad on his side, curled into her the way they slept when I was a kid.

When I get home, I go to wordsmith.org and check anagrams for CECIL VOLK. Eight matches come up, the first being CLICK LOVE. How apt for my loving father who taught me how to use the computer. I check PATRICIA VOLK. I get sixteen pages, the most interesting are: IRK LATVIA COP, PRICK TO AVAIL, VITA LIP CROAK, and the stunning pronouncement CRAP VIA LIT OK.

Dad's determined to get better. He will get better. He knows this. He is a competitor. It's one more opponent, cancer of the blood.

Everybody has food ideas.

"Liverwurst. You don't have to chew it."

"Steak blood."

"Jell-O made with fruit syrup."

"Really soggy French toast with a lot of maple syrup."

"A chocolate malted is the single most fattening thing on earth."

We have to stoke him with calories.

Ice cream is one of Dad's favorite foods. He can work through a pint or two watching TV after dinner. In Publix, the local supermarket, we compare calorie counts. We want the ice cream with the highest. Edy's Chocolate Fudge Mousse is only 160 a serving. Turkey Hill Chocolate Peanut Butter Cup, 180. Friendly's Reese's Pieces comes in at 230. Who knew ice cream was so dietetic? I reach for the Haagen-Dazs Chocolate, 270! Now we're getting somewhere. Ben & Jerry's Peanut Butter Cup wins at 380. Mom has gone from "Cecil, stop putting that in your mouth!" to "Cecil, please put that in your mouth!" with no intermission.

"I don't want anyone to mention food around me," Dad announces. "Please."

We try to stop, but how can he rally if he doesn't eat?

My sister goes into the guest bedroom, where Dad and his full-time nurse, Donna Claire, sleep. It's the room I usually stay in, a room that says End of the Millennium in Boca Raton, Florida. It has eighteen-foot ceilings and eleven walls and a porthole in the giant closet for viewing palms as you dress.

Donna Claire takes flawless care of Dad. He teases her. "She beats me with a rubber hose so the marks won't show," he says. "She does it when no one's looking. On the bottom of my feet." Donna cracks up. "She's vicious. A *killer.*"

My sister goes into the room. She's there a long time. I peek in. She's on the bed, facing Dad.

Later I ask. "What were you doing in there?"

"Visualization," she says. "Meditation technique. Hypnosis."

"Did he respond?"

"He cried."

"Oh, no!" I burst into tears. I've never seen my father cry.

We heat the water to ninety degrees. Dad feels good in the pool. It's the place where, weightless, he's most like he used to be. But he's caught in a trap. The more he exercises, the more oxygenated blood he uses up. Dad needs to exercise. It's what makes him feel good. But in the end, it will make him feel worse. On a good day, because you can't count on anything for more than a day, Dad will go in the pool twice. He'll float on his back with his arms looped under a long Styrofoam pool noodle. I noodle alongside him and make up a song:

> *When I swim in the pool with my Dad*
> *There is nothing that makes me so glad*
> *We'll swim and we'll play*
> *Throughout the whole day*

Then Dad supplies the last line:

> *Now what about that could be bad?*
> Or *With nothing to make us feel sad.*
> Or *Until your dear mother gets mad.*

We'll laugh until Mom uses her "You bad boy!" voice and tells him it's time to come out.

"Now?" Dad says. He's having fun. But Mom knows. He's using up good blood drifting around.

Dad pulls himself up the pool steps and collapses in his waterproof wheelchair. His chin falls on his chest. Donna showers and soaps him with warm water from a sprayer. Tenderly, she dabs 45 SPF sunblock cream on his newly hairless head.

When Dad embarks on a new chemo, when all his white blood cells or red cells or blast cells or whatever Dr. Harris is trying to kill at the moment get killed, at Dad's lowest point, we wear masks and gowns, wash our hands with bactericide, take our street shoes off, and don't let our skin come in contact with his. His immunity is zero. He has no resistance. But if I suck my breath in, the mask conforms to my lips and I can kiss him through the mask and it feels like a kiss. Dad loves kisses. He loves to be touched.

After a particularly brutal chemo, Dad says he will be happy again when he can watch TV and read the newspaper. He needs strength to watch TV. He needs strength to open his eyes. Mom and I test-drive some La-Z-Boy chairs so Dad can sit comfortably in front of the TV when he's up to it.

The La-Z-Boy becomes command central. Freddie, the gardener whose daughter Dad's helping through school, drifts in and discusses trimming the banana trees and new plants for the front.

"Pull out all the stops, Freddie," Dad says. "I want it gorgeous for Audrey."

The Boca Boys—Dad's Tuesday buddy group—trickle in. When Dad moved to Boca, he found three comrades right away. Dad, Aaron, Milton, and Arnold called themselves Bunk 4. They were going to have fun together, like in camp. Dad welded them iridescent BUNK 4 license plates for their cars. Every Tuesday they'd meet and vote on where to go for the cheapest lunch. Then they'd see a Jean-Claude Van Damme or Jackie Chan movie their wives would never sit through.

Word gets out. Bunk 4 touches a nerve. The group swells to seventeen and meets every Tuesday in Dad's kitchen. They change their name from Bunk 4 to the Boca Boys. On odd-numbered Tuesdays they wear black tennis shirts with the BOCA BOYS logo embroidered over their hearts. On even Tuesdays, red. They have matching baseball caps with the logo too. And engraved Swiss army knives. The Boca Boys get written up in the *Florida Sun-Sentinel:* "Volk calls the meeting of the group to order with several clangs of a brass bell he welded himself. He admits it's not an easy bunch to pull together. 'We got half a dozen conversations going on here at once,' said Volk, clanging the bell and calling for order a second time. 'Okay, what movie are we going to see? How about *No Escape* with Ray Liotta?' "

After the Boca Boys vote on the movie, they fan their discount lunch coupons all over Dad's kitchen table. Every week they pick the biggest, cheapest meal you can get for under four dollars. That's a founding Boca Boys principle. After the vote they thunder out in packed cars and seventeen laughing white-haired men storm an IHOP or a Bagelworks or a deli that has soup and a sandwich and a bottomless soft drink for $3.49. If nothing in the paper appeals, there is always the foot-long hot dog for a dollar at Costco. The consensus is the foot-long Costco dollar dog may be the bargain of the century. Whenever Dad picks me up at the airport, as soon as we hit Powerline Road, his eyes light, he leans over and says, "Wanna foot-long hot dog at Costco?" The Boca Boys eat lunch early. They want to make the empty noon show at the movies so every boy gets an aisle seat.

D ad's used to being in control. He keeps hoping. We all do. My sister gives him Meditapes, powerful visualization tapes she narrates for people going into surgery, insomniacs, people who have stress or are getting chemo. I bring Dad a boom box with George Shearing and Tito Puente CDs. My friend Kathy finds a recipe on the Internet for capsaicin candy, a hot-pepper candy that will relieve Dad's mouth. My sister consults her rabbi and a psychic: "Do you think he can get better?" Both agree he can. We go to her *shul* and pray. We get the whole *shul* to pray. We call all our doctor friends. Norm Gottlieb sends reprints from medical magazines. Michael Motro puts us in touch with the chemo pioneers in Israel and suggests we find out why Dad got this particular leukemia in the first place. Dad doesn't care, but I'd like to know. Next door to the store there was a dry cleaner, and the paper says exposure to dry-cleaning fumes can cause cancer. In the Twenty-eighth Street studio Dad shared with Zero Mostel, who was a serious painter and a passionate lover of Morgen's center-cut tongue sandwiches, Dad worked with chemicals. Maybe it was the patinas Dad used finishing sculptures in his studio at home. Maybe it was the hip radiation. Maybe he's living in the Love Canal of Florida. Even though there's a water filter under the kitchen sink, does it filter out everything? Thirty-eight states have poisoned water tables. A twelve-ounce bottle of Evian costs $1.25. A twelve-ounce Coke is 80 cents. Why does water cost more than Coke? Soon water will cost more than wine. They'll date the bottles so when you sip the water, you can say, "Ah, 1994 Crystal Geyser. A good year. That was before the nuclear waste dump polluted the Eastern Sierra." Seventy-three percent of all cancers are environmental. I don't trust the water my parents drink. Not a bit.

We surf the health Net. We keep believing we can make Dad better. It's a family trait. We don't relish problems, but we're good at tackling them. We never give up. Give us a problem, give us *cancer,* we rise. Dad will take any treatment out there. He'll try anything.

Each time I fly to Florida, when I walk through the front door, I look to my right toward the kitchen. The first good sign is Dad in the La-Z-Boy. If he isn't there, he's in bed—the first bad sign. His condition is read, reread, poured over, dissected. Breaths are analyzed. Everything is a clue, a reason to hope or worry.

"Does he look better to you?"

"I think so. Does he look better to you?"

"I don't know. You really think he looks better?"

"I don't know."

"Did he finish the egg?"

"All but a little."

When Mom skins her shin on the Formica corner of Dad's platform bed, he gets cranky. Cranky! He *is* getting better! I fold a washcloth in half and secure it to the protruding corner with duct tape. An inventor's daughter does this without thinking. Problem? Solution. Dad's house is filled with the jury-rigged. Five bathrooms have eyeglass cases Velcroed to the side of the vanity. The washer-dryer used to dance and rattle until Dad bumpered it with carpet scraps screwed on two-by-fours. Old tennis-ball cans corral TV zappers. The giant dictionary is always open on the stand made of stress rods kidnapped from construction sites. There is pretty much nothing on God's earth that can't be recycled or made better.

W hen you first learn you have cancer, you try to find the cure. When you can't find the cure, you hope for remission. When you can't hope for remission, you try for time. We are in the second phase.

Dad issues an edict. No one is to say, "How are you?"

"How do you *think* I am? Knucklehead."

I ask my sister how she feels when Dad calls her Lardass or Knucklehead.

"He never has," she says.

"Dad," I ask him, "how come you call me Lardass and Knucklehead and you don't call Jo?"

"Your sister's sensitive," he says and we laugh. I'm not? I've come to think of Lardass and Knucklehead as endearments.

I get on the bed and hold Dad's hand. I kiss it. The shape of his head is a surprise. It's flatter in the back and, without hair, smaller. I know Dad has a small head because a few visits ago, when he was still well enough to climb the stairs to his office, he gave me his beloved Tyrolean hat. He looked me in the eyes and said, "Take good care of this, Patricia Gay." It is green felt with a green rope around the crown emblazoned with forty-four years of enameled and jeweled American Motorcycle Association membership pins and the Heinz pickle pin Dad bought Mom at the 1939 World's Fair in New York. I look like Zeppo in the hat. It perches on top of my hair. Maybe he's normal, and my head is huge.

M om has a friend who has a brother who has acute myelogenous leukemia too. He's a doctor who is seventy-six. He lives in California, and he's in remission. A time is set. The doctor calls. He's on the same protocol as Dad. He tells Dad he's skiing. Dad is cheered. Hope flares. On the way to Good Sam the next day, a car cuts us off. Dad glares at the driver and says, "I slapped his face with leather gloves. We meet at dawn tomorrow."

I go down on a Friday and come back on a Sunday. Dad and I sing in the pool. I pull him by the noodle. I tell him I'm going to buy him a bench in Central Park. I kiss him and love him up good. We watch *Judge Judy*, the *Antiques Road Show*, and his favorite, the Nature Channel. We see bears maul humans, moths making love, and a hippo going wild. During the National Cutting Horse Association Super Stakes Non-Pro Final, a palomino does something tricky. Dad perks up. "That horse recovers well," he says. Of another, he shakes his head, "That horse has no snap."

Monday, Dad goes to Dr. Harris, and Dr. Harris has good news. Dad doesn't need blood! Platelets are up! No transfusions! He can go home! But Monday night Mom doesn't like the way he looks. Tuesday morning they drive back to Good Sam, Dad in the back, his head on a pillow on Donna's lap. The techs take blood. Dad's admitted. I cross off the latest DAD IN HOSP. phone number in my book and write in 835-2487.

I dial Dad the next morning. "What's going on, Dad?"

"How . . . are . . . you . . . Patricia Gay?"

"I miss you, Daddy."

"Forgive . . . me . . . I . . . have . . . to . . . speak . . . slowly. . . . My . . . tongue . . . is . . . swollen."

"Want me to do the talking, Daddy?"

"Yes . . . I . . . love . . . to . . . hear . . . your . . . voice. . . . You . . . talk."

I talk. I ramble. I sing. Singing is something we love doing together. In the car we sing Alphabet Geography. The first song is usually "Stars Fell on Alabama." Then it's "Bamy Bound" or "Brazil." Then "Nothing Could Be Fina Than to Be in Carolina in the Mor-or-or-ning." Sometimes we sing a moon medley: "By the Light of the Silvery Moon," "It's Only a Paper Moon," "Moon Over Miami," "That Ole Devil Moon." Sometimes we only sing songs about love: "Love, Your Magic Spell Is Everywhere," "I

Love You a Bushel and a Peck," "That's Amore." Today I sing my
father's favorite song, "Younger Than Springtime." When I finish, he doesn't say anything, but I can hear him breathing.

"I love you, Dad," I say.

"I . . . love . . . you . . . too."

That afternoon my sister calls. "I don't like the way Mom
sounds," she says. "I think you should get down here."

"What does she sound like?"

"Bad."

I call Dad again. The nurse picks up. "I'm Mr. Volk's daughter.
May I speak to him?"

"Mr. Volk is unable to speak."

"Why?"

"His tongue is swollen."

"Could you put the phone by his ear? Hello, Dad? It's Patty,
Dad. Can you hear me?"

"Mmm-hmm."

"I'm coming down, Dad. I'll be on the next plane. I'm gonna
sleep at the hospital tonight and keep you company. Okay, Dad?"

The nurse takes back the phone and tells me he smiled.

I get to the hospital at eleven. I kiss him and pull a chair up to
his bed so if he opens his eyes, he'll see me. I whisper to him, but
there's no response. Then he opens his eyes. I'm not sure if he
sees me. His eyes are cloudy, and they don't move. I lean back in
my chair and hold his hand. After a while he pulls his away. I
hold it again until he pulls it away again.

The room is dark. The only illumination is street fluorescence
angling through the venetian blinds. Suddenly Dad shoots up in
bed. "No!" he screams. The watery light reduces his face to white
and shadow. His mouth and eye sockets are black holes.

"What is it, Dad? What's the matter?"

I try to soothe him, but he falls back against his pillows and
closes his eyes. A little later, moving stronger and faster than he
has in a year, Dad hurls his legs off the bed. The night nurse,
who's been sleeping in a chair, races over and clamps her hands
on Dad's shoulders. She forces him down.

"Let him stand! He has to stand! His legs hurt!" I say.

I remember from childhood Dad bolting out of bed to walk off leg cramps. Even though he wore Murray Space Shoes in the store and took potassium pills, a restaurant man on his feet twelve hours a day gets leg cramps at night.

"You can't walk, Mr. Volk!" the nurse screams right in his ear.

"Yes, he can! You've got to let him!" I scream back.

"He's been in bed for two days. He'll fall. *Down*, Mr. Volk!"

"Get a walker! Get an orderly! I'll help! You have to let him walk. *Please.*"

Dad pushes against her, but the nurse wins. I run to the nurses' station and tell them my father wants to walk, needs to walk, *has* to walk.

"We can't let him do that," the nurse says without looking up. "He'll fall and break a hip."

"Not if we support him! He's in pain! You need to let him put weight on his feet! You HAVE to!"

Is there no way on earth to let my father safely stand? Have they given up? Don't they care anymore?

Later Dad bolts up again. Again he swings his legs over. I beg the nurse. She wrestles him down for the second time. I'm failing my father. I know I am. My brain isn't working. I'm desperate. I can't think of any way to help him. If the tables were turned, he would have found a way to let me stand. The inventor's daughter can't invent a way to help her father.

"At least give him something for pain," I say. They do. He goes to sleep, and I stare at the face I love so much, and the only way I get through the night, what saves me from becoming a sobbing primal wreck on the floor, is thinking about the snow chair. Forty-something years ago we woke up one Sunday and the world was white. We put on our leggings and walked across the street to Riverside Park. Some kids were there with their mothers, some with their fathers. The kids with fathers were making snowmen. Dad began packing the snow. We helped, scooping up armloads. He'd tell us where to drop them. He worked hard, laughing, bending over, shaping it. When he was finished, a giant upholstered armchair overlooked the Hudson. We took turns sitting in it, legs dangling, watching snow-covered ice floes wade down the river. The snow chair, our snow throne. We rarely took a camera. My only record of the snow chair is in my head. I haven't thought of the snow chair in years. But tonight it comes back, and I relive the feeling of unadulterated joy, the miracle of my father and his imagination. I loop snow-chair footage in my head over and over and over. We wake up. The world is white. We go out. Dad builds the chair. We sit in it. Over and over so that when I look at my father in the bed, I see him in his camel-hair coat and galoshes, roses in his cheeks. When I start to bawl, I say to myself, "Snow chair, snow chair. Snow chair."

In the morning Mom and my sister get to the hospital at seven. Dad is unresponsive. At ten thirty Dr. Harris makes rounds. He puts his ear on my father's chest and looks in his eyes. Then he comes out of the room and talks to us.

"He's dying," the doctor says, avoiding my mother's eyes. "I think he may have had a small stroke. If I took a picture of his head, I'm fairly sure I would see he'd bled into his brain."

"Are you saying you want him to go downstairs for some X rays?" Mom asks hopefully.

"No."

Dr. Harris tells us he's going to give Dad morphine.

Someone says, "How long?"

"Two or three days."

They hook Dad up to the morphine. We sit by his bed till the four-o'clock night nurse comes on. At one point Mom leans over Dad, whispers something in his ear, and he smiles. Over and over, all day, she keeps saying to him, "Dr. Harris is coming with something new. Some magic, sweetheart. Dr. Harris has something magic for you, Cecil. It's on the way." She smoothes her hand over his head and trails her fingers. It's something my father must have loved. We all kiss him. My sister wants to sleep in Dad's room, but we convince her to come home. At night we share a bed. We hold hands and cry.

At 4:45 the phone rings. My sister runs into my mother's room. When she comes back to where I am, she stands over the bed and says, "He's dead."

I can't speak.

"Do you hear me, Patty? He's dead."

It's July fourteenth. It's Bastille Day. The moon is still up. We drive to the hospital.

In his room Dad is lying with the covers pulled under his chin. His eyes are closed. You can see his teeth a little. We sit with him. We each take a few minutes with him alone. We kiss him. He's not cold, but he is damp. We hold his hand. We talk to him. We sit without speaking, then Mom says we have to go. I don't want to go. I want to be with him. Mom says, "We have to go now. Bad things start happening soon. Come, girls. We have to go."

A nurse stops us in the hall, says she's sorry, and asks about donating Dad's body to science.

"He's been cut up enough already," Mom says.

Another nurse tells us Dad wasn't alone when he died, that she and a couple of other nurses were there. He wasn't awake. He wasn't in pain. He simply stopped breathing. They had told us Dad would have two or three days once they started the morphine. My sister will not forgive herself for not spending the night.

Back at the house, Mom asks her to leave a message on the phone: "Cecil succumbed to leukemia at four forty-five this morning. I will return your call at a later date."

She doesn't want anyone around but the immediate family, the sixteen of us. We're not sitting shivah. We're not saying *Kaddish*. Dad didn't want us to. Mom asks her grandson John to go up to Dad's office and delete all the files in his computer.

My sister and I put on bathing suits. We need to move. We dive into the pool. Without discussing it, we scull ourselves downward. Sitting on the bottom, legs akimbo, we serve each other tea underwater, pouring from an invisible pot into invisible cups. We sip. Then we burst out of the water laughing wildly. We go down again and touch tongues. We haven't done this since 1953.

Condolence letters pour in. Dad meant something to people we had no idea he knew. There are loving letters from bank tellers, waiters, and car repairmen. His poetry teachers, artists, the children of friends. We get two hundred and forty-six letters.

"Look at all these people who cared about Dad," I say to Mom.

"Your father felt very welcome in the world," she says.

When his obit comes out in the paper, a new wave of letters arrives. The obit captures Dad. It captures the high times at Morgen's. It calls the store "a garment district social center for decades." It describes Dad's inventions and how he met Mom. It gets one thing wrong. It says Dad "perfected the art of the schmooze." But Dad was too deeply private to authentically schmooze. "When you tell someone about yourself, you give them power over you," he'd say. Dad rarely spoke about himself. He had a joke or a story tailored for everyone. It made people laugh while it gave him distance. The obit ends with a quote from my mother: " 'Everybody seemed to think he was their best friend,' " Mrs. Volk said. 'Anybody he touched was very happy. It's a known fact.' "

Two weeks after Dad dies, my nephew John picks up his ashes. The crematologist calls them cremains. He says he's never felt such heavy ones. We speculate it's Dad's titanium hip. My sister wants some of the ashes to bury. Her rabbi has told her it's okay to do that if it will make her feel better. "You have to respect your mom on this," he adds. I tell my sister what Tolstoy said: "The body is just an overcoat for the soul."

We are going to scatter Dad in the Atlantic. We board our friend Jim's boat. Mom sits portside embracing the box. She's huddled over it. No one speaks. Jim puts Mozart on the CD player. The sun is setting. We've told Mom what Dad asked us to do. We've told her he designed heart lockets for us to put a bit of his ashes in. Lockets we can wear and always have him with us. But Mom wants all of him together. When we get to 25°38.552N by 80°11.863W, when we no longer see land, at that precise point we take turns scattering Dad from a deck off the stern while the sun goes down. My nephew Michael grips the back of our shirts so we don't fall overboard. The ashes are not like I've read about. They're not brown or greasy. They are cement gray with shards of white and black in them. When it's my turn, I watch them cloud out in the water, and when I raise the plastic bag, the ashes in the neck of it are so heavy they don't go back in the bag. They spill all over my feet. I try to scoop them up. "I'm sorry I'm sorry I'm sorry I'm sorry I'm sorry," I keep saying while Michael hoses them off. I lose track of time. Someone pulls me back to my seat. Mom goes last. She seems so fragile, so newly small.

My sister and I look at each other. I lick my hand. She licks hers. The sun is down. We head back. We dock and go out to a place Dad liked for dinner. A few days later, before I leave for New York, Mom and I head for our favorite beach at Red Reef. We plow through the waves, and I think about the summer the four of us vacationed on the Lido. Dad loved the Adriatic. It was warm and clear. He loved the little crabs in the shallow water. "Granchi," he called them, and teased my mother. "You're a *vecchio* granchi," he'd say, and laugh.

Mom and I bob in the ocean. It's like the butterfly flapping its wings in Japan. Over time the breeze wafts all over the world. Anything you put in water anywhere eventually makes its way into every drop of water on the planet. We're swimming with Dad. Mom and I talk and drift. We have a good time.

B ack in New York, it's my sister on the phone.
"I miss him," I say.
She gasps, then goes silent. Finally she says, "I can't believe you're saying that. That's so the *least* of it."

Does my sister think my grief is less than profound?

I put on my running shoes and go to the park. I look for a bench for Dad. Every bench in Central Park has a number on the back, and if it's still available, you can buy it and have a personalized plaque screwed on the front. I walk by the tennis courts. Dad loved tennis. He loved to play it and to watch it. But these benches aren't in great shape and they're right up against a chain-link fence. I find a brand-new bench I like beautifully shaded near a fountain, but when I call the Central Park Conservancy, I learn all the benches in that area are reserved for Helen Frankenthaler, who has given the park $100,000. I set out again. I want a bench on my beaten path, a bench I can sit on every day, a bench with meaning.

I narrow the benches down to two. One is by the south gatehouse, but the view is partially obstructed. I decide to go with the bench next to Madeline Kahn's, where the bridle path meets the reservoir track and the drive just north of the West Side entrance to the Eighty-sixth Street transverse. People pour into the park here. The views are west, where we lived, east, where I live now, and the bench faces downtown, where Dad worked. The bridle path is where Mom and Dad used to ride on weekends, and I can sit on this bench every morning when I walk around the reservoir. Two London plane trees frame the view.

Mom dictates the plaque:

IN LOVING MEMORY OF
CECIL S. VOLK
AUDREY PATRICIA JO ANN

There are little hearts between our names.

When Mom comes up for Thanksgiving, I take her to see the bench. The one to Dad's left has been sold. That plaque honors the Starrett family, the people who built the Municipal Building on the land Jacob Volk cleared.

Mom sits on Dad's bench. We chat. She tells me that after she broke her back on the bridle path, after it healed, Dad took her to a dude ranch to practice getting thrown. "We'd go every weekend," Mom says. "I had to keep falling off so I'd learn the right way to fall off and never break my back again."

I tell her when I think of Dad going to the hospital for transfusions, I'm not sad. "People were always so happy to see him," I say.

"He enjoyed getting everyone under his spell," my mother says. "He interacted to the end."

A runner comes by and we ask her to take our picture with our arms curled above the plaque. As we get up to go, Mom studies Dad's bench in relation to his neighbors'. She takes the three benches in and says, "Why did they have to put dates on Madeline Kahn's? And the Starrett family! Look at all those words. It's overwritten. Our bench is the best."

Grief is a surprise. It's not a long wailing process that gradually tapers off. The intensity of it comes and goes. Remembering good things is purely joyful. There's *laughter*. I don't feel loss all the time, because my father is vivid and in so much I do. How I dice. How I make knots. Clipping my toenails his prescribed way. (You never know how strange your family is until you see the expression on someone's face when you say, "My father always cuts my toenails. He doesn't trust other people.") When something breaks, Dad's on my shoulder, saying, "Study how it works!" or "Get out the manuals!" (stored in a labeled MANUALS file). I look up words in the dictionary, finding winsome new ones on the way. Since he cared deeply about the edge on knives, since every time he came to visit, the first thing he'd do was walk into my kitchen and check my knives against the pillow of his thumb, I get them professionally sharpened and check them against my thumb. When I look in the mirror, he's there smiling back. Much of the time it feels as if Dad's with me. "My heart with pleasure fills." I fall apart only when I think of him perplexed and suffering. Thinking of that whacks me like a bat behind the knees.

"When someone dies, you don't cry for them," Professor Fred Haaucke told our aesthetics class. "They're dead. You cry for *you*." I'd hoped this was true. It's not. I don't cry for me because I miss him. I cry for how Dad suffered.

When I was growing up, I had three hobbies. I collected stamps, tropical fish, and bugs. All three are microcosms. Stamps are miniature portraits, landscapes, and historical reenactments. *Washington Crossing the Delaware* an inch big is a defining moment in history smaller than your toe. A tropical fish aquarium is a universe complete with birth and death and evolution, all right on top of your dresser. And bugs, how they move and behave, how they interact, what they do to survive, and how they plod on no matter what, are microscopic role models. Microcosms fascinate because they tell big stories on an accessible scale. They are worlds you can hold in your hand. Now I collect snow globes, three-inch cities in perpetual blizzards. But my most interesting microcosm is the one I was born with, family. Family is what we first know of the world. Family *is* the world, your very own living microcosm of humanity, with its heroes and victims and martyrs and failures, beauties and gamblers, hawks and lovers, cowards and fakes, dreamers and steamrollers, and the people who quietly get the job done. Every behavior in the world is there to watch at the dinner table. You study them. You learn. You see how they change and how they stay the same. But if you think you can really know them, you're missing the point. The point isn't how well you know somebody. The point is this: In a family you don't come from nowhere. You enter the world already part of something. The myths and behaviors are all there to model yourself on or against. You are who you came from. There is no escape, but there is transmutation. Family is how you become who you will be. It's through family you learn there are no limits on ideas, nothing is strange if it seems right, and if you believe in what you do, who cares what anybody else thinks. Knowing so much about them, how open-hearted can you bear to be? You were born with the chance to love them. You might as well. They're yours.

Cecil Sussman Volk in full regalia

STEAMERS

Dad raises his chin and buckles his helmet. He zips his black leather jacket, the one with the new gusset in the back. He pulls on the black leather gloves with the flared cuffs and flexes his fingers. He swings his leg over the bike, forwards his weight to lift the kickstand, then revs.

Vroom, VROOM. *VROOOOOOOM.*

He adjusts the gas. The bike is roaring. He flips his face mask down and nods for me to hop on. It's Sunday. He can't find some papers. We're going to the store for the last time.

The Long Island Expressway is wide-open. We sail into the city, past Lefrak "If You Lived Here, You'd Be Home by Now" City, past the expanding and contracting propane tank and the cemetery where Dad likes to note, "People are dying to get in there," until the skyline rises, surprising yet familiar every time.

Dad parks the bike in front of the store, and we go in through the side entrance. It's dark and quiet. We head upstairs through the secret door. The walls of Morgen's are booked mahogany to the ceiling, where they meet a dentil molding. Set in one page of the mahogany is a knobless interior-hinged door you wouldn't know was there unless you knew it was there. Behind the secret door, to the right, are a desk and a phone where Dad negotiates orders for the day, books parties, takes reservations. To the left a narrow staircase twists up to a room that has a twenty-foot desk and a six-foot safe at the far end. Like the downstairs desk, it's covered with piles of paper, drifts and stacks, papers on spindles. Bad checks are taped to the wall.

Morgana meows. The stray cat Dad rescued lives in the office. Dad once wanted to be a veterinarian. Dogs and cats sense his goodwill. In a roomful of people he's the first to get nuzzled. Morgana is fat and glossy. Dad's brought her back to life. She tucks through his ankles.

There's a quarter-inch hole in the east wall of the office. You can peep through it and check out the floor. The accountants and the biller work up here. It's where cash is kept and where Dad hides his Smith & Wesson .38 Chiefs Special Revolver Model No. 36 and his Hi-Standard .22 Long Rifle with Supermatic Citation that he uses for target practice. He carries the .38 when he goes to the bank. With the advent of plastic, there's not that much money. But there's still enough and you don't have to be a genius to know that when Cecil Volk of Morgen's is speed-walking down Broadway, he's got cash.

Dad sifts through some papers. I remember the Sunday I rode in with him after the police called to say the store had been robbed. It was the only time I saw the safe open with its smaller safe inside. I remember lunches up here because the store was so packed, they couldn't spare a table. I'd eat my club sandwich at the desk, playing with the adding machine and the magnetized paper-clip holder.

Dad can't find what he's looking for. He strokes Morgana and turns out the light. We walk through the silent restaurant, a graveyard of red leather chairs upended on tables. Dad threads his way easily to the other staircase near the hatcheck booth, where the concessionaire sold fat cigars, Sen-Sen, and the

strangest-tasting mint in the world—C. Howard's Violet, lilac
squares wrapped in purple foil that tasted like flowers.

The wide terrazzo stairs lead to the subterranean Morgen's. It's
bigger than the main floor and reserved for private bookings. It
was here I had my sixth-grade birthday party. Three tables were
set in a U, as if it were a testimonial dinner. On top of white table-
cloths, forming a green U inside the linen U, Dad laid a spine of
ferns. My class had burgers. Later we walked to Times Square,
and I got my first kiss. Richie Mishkin slung his arm around my
neck and pulled my head toward his. We documented the
moment in a photo booth for proof.

Downstairs, Dad leads me to a place I've never seen, a low-
ceilinged storage area. While he looks for the missing papers, he
says to me, "Take anything you want."

The store has been sold. Not the store exactly, but the lease to
the store, a lease Dad worked two tough years negotiating. An
Italian restaurant is moving in. In four years it will be in the
newspapers. A woman in a red Mercedes will drive through the
plate-glass window at 141 West Thirty-eighth Street and kill a
customer at table 3, the small booth to the left of the entrance
where Mom and Dad used to have coffee before the lunch crush.
The Italian restaurant is subletting the store from Dad. It was a
good move negotiating that lease. It's income. When Uncle Bob
closed Morgen's East, that was it, his lease was up.

Dad's bike has two saddlebags. I can't take too much. I look for
things that will last, so my home will never be without stuff from
the store. I look for infinite shelf life, a lifetime supply of something. I take one-pound containers of dry mustard, paprika, and
cinnamon. I take two thousand lamb-chop panties, one bag gold,
one white. I take a box of one thousand Morgen's cellophane-
frilled toothpicks and a box of five hundred Stir-eo Straws my
kids will love, a box of one hundred silver petit-four moules and
two gallons of nonpareils, tiny beads of colored sugar the kids eat
on yogurt, on *anything*. When I want Polly and Peter to eat their
vegetables, I sprinkle them with Morgen's nonpareils. I take a
mason jar of Morgen's seasoning salt.

"May I have something from the kitchen, Dad?"

He's already set me up with knives. I take the enormous wooden salad bowl my favorite Morgen's chopped chef salad was chopped in. This bowl will take up a whole saddlebag, but I love it. It has a honey patina and more crosshatches than a Dürer. I am sure this bowl, like Mom's chopped-egg bowl, imparts flavor. I take two restaurant-grade saucepans, the sloping dull metal kind with thick pitted stay-cool handles riveted to the sides. From behind the bar I take a round cocktail strainer and a long spoon the bartender uses to swizzle drinks. It has a red plastic ball on top, and the shaft is turned like a drill bit. I don't make mixed drinks, but I've only seen a spoon like this at Morgen's. I pack up two cartons of Morgen's matches and a few menus.

I don't like lasts. Even if I am moving to an apartment with more room, a bigger and better apartment, I'm sad leaving the old place. "This is the last time I will cook oatmeal on this stove." "This is the last time I will use this tub." "This is the last time I'll come home from this particular job with my children racing to this particular door." "This is the last time I'll wake up with the sun hitting my face this particular way." It doesn't matter if what I'm headed for is better. It's about a thing disappearing. Something will never be again.

So the last Morgen's is closing. When Dad locks the doors for the last time, the hundred-year story of our New York restaurant family is *fini*. From Sussman Volk in 1888 to Cecil Sussman Volk in 1988. One complete century. This last store was the hub of the garment center in the hub of the city in the hub of the nation that's the hub of the planet. Mom and Dad fed the people that clothed the country when MADE IN AMERICA was the label of choice. It was a place that gave good value. A place where people knew that a family was there and they'd knock themselves out to take care of you. Whether they were working during the day or having a bite before the theater, customers could count on a sprawling menu filled with freshly prepared first-rate imaginative food. For one hundred years our family fed New York. In my fraction of that time I've lost lots of restaurants: Schrafft's, the Automat, the counter at Henry Halper's, Mary Elizabeth's, Le Pavillon, Charda's, the vegetable plate at the New York Women's Exchange. I've lost stores too, the three B's: Best's, Bonwit's, and B. Altman's. And customs: wearing gloves to walk down Fifth Avenue, *wanting* to walk down Fifth Avenue, *bon voyage* parties, crinolines, children playing potsy on the sidewalk, jump seats in cabs. We listened to the *Victrola*. We packed our clothes in a *valise*. And even though it ran on electricity, we stored our food in the *icebox*. Photos of my grandfathers are starting to look young. Even Bing Crosby's starting to look young. One generation ago, four generations met weekly for dinner. Now those people live in Honolulu, Scottsdale, and Boca Raton.

The restaurant business, feeding people, will always be a way to make a living. To make extra money in college both my children get their bartending licenses. While continuing his studies, Peter mans the bar at The Conservatory in the Mayflower Hotel on Central Park West. At night he waits tables at Farfalle on Columbus Avenue. Polly, my daughter, gets a job hostessing at Restaurant Daniel. When she seats people (like her Great-great-grandpa Louis, her Great-grandma Polly, and my mother), they eagerly press fifty- or hundred-dollar bills in her hand. Before dinner starts Polly answers the phone. "Zees eez Dahn-yell-uh," Bruno has told her to say. "Ow may I elp you?"

But just when I think our family is out of the food business, my sister's husband opens a New York–style food store called JoAnna's Marketplace in Coral Gables. In JoAnna's first year of business Alan wins the *Miami Herald*'s first prize for his Chocolate Decadence Cake with a ganache so rich yet light it seems like a new category of food. His sons, Michael and John, go into JoAnna's with him. They marry, and Kelly and Tonya go in too. Like the tables our family sets, JoAnna's Marketplace has room for everybody. Now Alan and the boys have opened another

JoAnna's in the Grove. On Thanksgiving, JoAnna's bastes four hundred turkeys and opens its doors at five a.m. A restaurant closes. A food store opens. We're still feeding people.

P atricia Gay?" Dad calls in the dark. He's found the papers. We ride home on the bike. On the way he turns his head sideways and yells, "Want some lunch?"

"Sure," I yell back.

He passes the turnoff for Kings Point and heads for Port Washington. Last time in store, last Louie's for clams. We order two large bowls of steamers. We pull them out of the shells by their muscular black siphons, swish them free of sand in briny broth, then dip them in a bowl of clarified butter. We bite their rubbery necks off.

"You realize you're eating a whole animal," Dad says.

"Stomach, heart, mouth, foot, esophagus, gills, mantle, digestive system, and everything that implies, Dad."

"Well, at least they're dead. When you eat raw clams and oysters, they're still alive."

We toss the empty shells in the big bowl between us. I look out on the town dock, a favorite make-out place where grinning police liked to tap the fogged-up windows and say, "Does your mother know you're here?"

Careful not to disturb silt that's settled on the bottom, we sip the gray broth. "Did you know, there are over twelve thousand species of clams?"

"No, Dad."

"Mollusks are bivalves," he continues. "*Bivalvia.* See this horny ligament? It works like a hinge to let the shells open. And these?" He points to thready nuggets still stuck on the dorsal interior of the shells. "These are the adductor muscles. They're too small to eat in a steamer, but scallops are adductor muscles. We're eating soft-shell clams, *Mya arenaria.* Do you know how they reproduce, Petroushka?"

"Tell me."

"The female releases eggs into the water. The male releases sperm. Somehow they find each other."

"I'm glad I'm not a clam, Dad."

"Me too."

As we wipe the butter off our chins, Dad says, "Did I ever tell you sailors chew clamshells for calcium?"

We head for home. Dad's a careful but aggressive motorcyclist. He believes in driving offensively. We swerve in and out of traffic, not for the thrill but because the car in front of us is being driven with less than optimum skill. It's too slow, too erratic (the geezer phenomenon), fails to observe a signal. It's a late braker, an early braker, a stuttering braker, a bobber and weaver, any one of the countless things the motorist in front of a biker can do wrong.

The wind whips down the neck of my jacket. The sun warms my face. It's a gorgeous day. What clouds there are look like gauze. I have two choices on the bike: I can hold on to the strap that bisects the seat. Or I can put my arms around my father's waist. I opt for his waist. We lean left. We lean right. We get so close to other cars I see eyebrows rise. Horns honk. Drivers shout. Somebody shoots us the bird. Cars peel out of our path, the road opens wide. We lean so low into a curve I see flecks of mica in the blacktop. And I feel the way I always feel with my father, safe.

DIRECTORIES

1887 NEW YORK CITY DIRECTORY
LIEBAN Louis furs, 28 Spring, h.177 Delancey

1897 NEW YORK CITY DIRECTORY
LIEBAN Louis clerk H.323 E. 89
VOLK Sussman provns 86 1/2 Delancey h.118 Orchard

1901 NEW YORK CITY DIRECTORY
LIEBAN Louis clerk, 1836 Madison
VOLK Sussman provns 86 1/2 Delancey
VOLK Albert wheelwright h.302 Morris av

1905 NEW YORK CITY DIRECTORY
LIEBAN Louis agent h.1618 Washington av
VOLK Sussman provns 88 Delancey
VOLK Albert wheelwright h. 681 Washington av

1910 NEW YORK CITY DIRECTORY
LIEBAN Louis buyer 2466 Marion av
MORGENBESSER Herman meat 805 Columbus av h.103W100th
VOLK Albert A contractor 56 Beaver R41 h.88 Delancey
VOLK Jacob contractor 56 Beaver R41&266West h. 88 Delancey
VOLK Sussman provns 88 Delancey

1915 NEW YORK CITY DIRECTORY
LIEBAN Elias dentist 95 Fox
LIEBAN Louis slsmn h.95 Fox
MORGENBESSER Leopold lab h.200avC
  (N–Z is missing from The New York Public Library)

1916 NEW YORK CITY DIRECTORY

LIEBAN Louis mlnr 922E163d h.1041 Hoe av
   Elias dentist 940 Fox r1041 Hoe av
   Gertrude slswmn r1041 Hoe av
   Jerome slsmn r1041 Hoe av
VOLK Albert A pres-treas Albert Volk & Co. h422S
VOLK JACOB HOUSEWRECKING CO INC (NY) Jacob Volk Pres;
   Housewreckers, Dealers in Building Material 103 Park
   av R217, Tel Murray Hill 292 (See adv in Building Material Dept)
VOLK Sussman provns 88 Delancey

1929 MANHATTAN WHITE PAGES/WINTER

LIEBAN E Alan Dr dntst 30W59 PLaza-4980
   r3671 Bway EDGecombe-8995
   Louis r3671 Bway EDGecombe-8995
HERMAN'S 133 W 38 St CORP 133W38 WISconsin-7590
MORGEN'S SANDWICH SHOPS INC. 1214 Bway BOGardus-8984
VOLK Albert A House Wrecking Co 1819 Bway COLumbus-7800
VOLK Jacob House Wrecking Co Inc 103 Park av ASHland-5166
VOLK Sussman provisns 88 Delncy ORChard-4843

1931 NEW YORK WHITE PAGES

LIEBAN E Alan Dr dntst 30W59 PLaza 3-4980
   Louis 10 Bennett av WAshHts 7-1624
MORGEN'S GRILL 176 5th av STuyvsnt 9-8427
MORGEN'S SANDWICH SHOPS INC. 1214 Bway BOgardus 4-8984
VOLK Albert A Co Inc hse wreckers&excavtrs 1819 Bway COlumbs 5-7800
VOLK Sussman Co provsns 88 Dlncy ORchard 4-4843

1933 NEW YORK WHITE PAGES/WINTER

HERMAN's CAFETERIA 6W32 LAckwana 4-3793
HERMAN'S COFFEE SHOPPE INC 145 Cedar WOrth 2-9812
HERMAN'S TAVERN 500 7av CHickrng 4-6988
LIEBAN E. Alan Dr dntst 30W59 PLaza 3-4980
   Louis 370 Ft. Wash av WAshHts 7-1624
VOLK Albert A Co Inc hse wreckers&excavtrs 1819 Bway COlumbs 5-7800
VOLK Jacob wrckrs 103 Pk av LExingtn 2-7659
VOLK Sussman delctsn 88 Dlncy Orchard 4-4843

1938 NEW YORK WHITE PAGES/SUMMER

HERMAN'S CAFETERIA 6W32 LAckwana 4-3793
LIEBAN E Alan Dr dntst 30W59 PLaza 3-4980
   Residence 411 WEndAv Traflgr 7-6772
   Louis 820 WendAv Acadmy 2-1530
MORGEN Herman 845 WEndAv Academy 2-1587

VOLK Albert A Co Inc hse wreckrs&excavtrs 1819 Bway COlumbs 5-7800
VOLK Ethel E 845 WEndAv Endicot 2-2746
VOLK Sussman Co delctsn 88 Dlncy Orchard 4-4843

1942–43 NEW YORK WHITE PAGES

HERMAN'S CAFETERIA 6W32 LAckwana 4-3793
  Public Tel 30W33
HERMAN'S Luncheonette 284 Prk WOrth 2-8086
LIEBAN E Alan Dr dntst 30W59 PLaza 3-4980
  Residence 140 RivDr
  Louis 820 WendAv ACadmy 2-1530
ROBERT'S BAKE SHOP 130 8th CHelsea 2-9818
ROBERT'S SEAFOOD 1147 Bway MUrryHill 4-9670
ROBERT'S TAVERN INC 1151 Bway MUrryhil 4-9787
VOLK Albert A Co Inc hse wreckrs&excavtrs 1819 Bway
VOLK Albert A Co Inc 871 5th Ave REgent 7-4180
  COlumbs 5-7800
VOLK Cecil 320 CentPkW SCuylr 4-3290
VOLK Sussman Co delcatesn 88 Dlncy ALgonqn 4-7377

1950 NEW YORK WHITE PAGES

LIEBAN E Alan Dr dntst 30W59 PLaza 3-4980
MORGEN'S Restrnt 141W38 LOngacr 3-7316
MORGEN Herman 565 WendAv ENdicot 2-2640
  Robert I 677 WEndAv
PENGUIN Refrigeration Co 188 6thAv WAlkr 5-7636
ROBERT'S BAKE SHOP 130 8th Chelsea 2-9618
STAVIN Nathan M DDS 51 W86 SChylr 4-1169
VOLK Albert A Co Inc hse wreckrs 1819 Bway COlumbs 5-7800
VOLK Cecil 110 RivDr SCuylr 4-3290
VOLK Sussman Co. delatesn 90 Delncy ALgonqn 4-8578
WOLKO TAILORS 37W125 LEhigh 4-9324

2001

LEDERMAN, Jo Ann Volk Coral Gables, Florida
LIEBAN, Richard Honolulu, Hawaii
MORGEN, Barbara Krass Scottsdale, Arizona
MORGEN, Hedy Toronto, Canada
VOLK, Audrey Morgen Boca Raton, Florida
VOLK, Patricia New York, New York